SALVATION
ON
SAND
MOUNTAIN

———

Also by
DENNIS COVINGTON

Lizard
Lasso the Moon

SALVATION

ON

SAND

MOUNTAIN

Snake Handling and Redemption

in Southern Appalachia

DENNIS COVINGTON

▲
▼▼

ADDISON–WESLEY PUBLISHING COMPANY

Reading, Massachusetts   Menlo Park, California   New York

Don Mills, Ontario   Wokingham, England   Amsterdam   Bonn   Sydney

Singapore   Tokyo   Madrid   San Juan   Paris   Seoul

Milan   Mexico City   Taipei

Portions of this work have appeared in different form in
The New York Times, The Chattahoochee Review, and on
National Geographic Explorer.

The epigraph is excerpted from "The Grotesque in Southern
Fiction" from *Mystery and Manners* by Flannery O'Connor and
edited by Sally and Robert Fitzgerald. Copyright © 1969 by the
Estate of Mary Flannery O'Connor. Reprinted by permission of
Farrar, Straus & Giroux, Inc.

This is a work of nonfiction, but memory is an imperfect guide.

Library of Congress Cataloging-in-Publication Data

Covington, Dennis.
    Salvation on Sand Mountain : snake handling and
redemption in southern Appalachia / by Dennis Covington.
        p.   cm
    ISBN 0-201-62292-0
        1. Snake cults (Holiness churches)—Southern States.
    2. Snake cults (Holiness churches)—Appalachian Mountains,
    Southern.   3. Southern States—Church history
    4. Appalachian Region—Church History   5. Covington,
    Dennis. I. Title.
    BX7990.H6C68   1995
    289.9—dc20   94-40335
                                                         CIP

Jacket design by Michael Ian Kaye
Jacket photographs by Jim Neel
Text design by Merrick Hamilton
Set in 10-point Sabon by Merrick Hamilton

1 2 3 4 5 6 7 8 9-DOC-97969594
First printing, December 1994

In memory of
SAM S. COVINGTON
my father

Contents

Acknowledgments

Special thanks to Don Fehr, my editor, who conceived this book and steered it to completion; to Vicki Covington, who took time away from her own garden to tend mine; and to artists Jim Neel and Melissa Springer, who shared the journey and whose photographs appear herein.

Thanks also to Rosalie Siegel, Paul Haskins, Bill Leonard, Ashley Covington, Laura Covington, Jeanie and Bunky Wolaver, Kat and Jack Marsh, Edna Covington, Cathy Jennings, Maxine Resnick, Judy Katz, Joey Kennedy, Katye Tipton, Walter and Eva Ruth Sisk, Cheryl Simonetti, William Hull, Tim Kelley, Dale Chambliss, Tom Camp, and Yvonne Crumpler and the staff of the Southern Collection of the Birmingham Public Library. I am particularly indebted to the work of David Hackett Fischer, Wayne Flynt, Harold Bloom, Thomas Burton, and David Kimbrough.

There are some acknowledgments for which thanks are not enough. May there be showers of blessings upon Carl Porter, my friend and spiritual mentor; and upon Carolyn Porter, Charles and Aline McGlocklin, J.L. Dyal, Elvis Presley Saylor, Cecil and Carolyn Esslinder, Gracie McAllister, Bobbie Sue Thompson, Bill Pelfrey, Daisy Parker, Dewey Chafin, Billy and Joyce Summerford, Punkin Brown, Allen Williams, Darlene Collins Summerford, Glenn Summerford, and all those others whose faith illuminates these pages.

This descent into himself will, at the same time, be a descent into his region. It will be a descent through the darkness of the familiar into a world where, like the blind man cured in the gospels, he sees men as if they were trees, but walking.

FLANNERY O'CONNOR,
Mystery and Manners

Prologue

This morning, on my way back from the mailbox, a neighbor asked whether I'd finished the new book. "Not quite," I said. I didn't have the heart to tell her I hadn't even begun.

"Well, I just wanted to know if you'd included anything about spirit trees," she said.

Spirit trees?

She explained what they were, bare trees in rural yards adorned with colored glass bottles. Then I remembered I'd seen them before. I thought they were only decorative. But my neighbor told me spirit trees had a purpose. If you happen to have evil spirits, you put bottles on the branches of a tree in your yard. The more colorful the glass, the better, I suppose. The evil spirits get trapped in the bottles and won't do you any harm. This is what Southerners in the country do with evil spirits.

The reason I didn't know much about spirit trees is that I'm a city boy. I was born, and still live, in Birmingham, an industrial city founded *after* the Civil War. My father, too, was born in Birmingham, in 1912, so he didn't know much about spirit trees, either. One of twelve children, he worked for the steel company most of his life and eventually died of emphysema.

I came of age reading the great Southern fiction of Faulkner, O'Connor, Welty, and Warren, but their South was not really a world I knew firsthand. I'd never plowed behind a mule or picked cotton or butchered a hog. And when I'd visit distant cousins in the country, they'd remind me of how little I knew about *real* life. To them, I was a city slicker. I wore pleated trousers instead of overalls.

The first fiction I wrote, though, had rural settings. My first published short story was called, curiously enough, "Salvation on Sand Mountain."

Fact is, twenty years ago I'd never even *been* on Sand Mountain, but I was drawing my material out of a rich Southern literature, the texture of which I'd never experienced myself. In time, the settings and people of my fiction began to resemble more and more those of the world I knew most intimately, the City. I started writing about urban couples, with or without children, and the minor perplexities they faced. The fiction seemed more honest to me, but something was missing. The stories might as well have been set in Portland or Des Moines. I started to wonder if I was still a Southern writer. I started to wonder if there was still a South at all.

In a 1990 *Time* essay, Hodding Carter III tells us there's not. "The South as South," he writes, "a living, ever regenerating mythic land of distinctive personality, is no more." But I wish Mr. Carter could have heard evangelist Bob Stanley's sermon at a snake-handling church in Kingston, Georgia, this past June: "Spread the word! We're coming off the farm! We're coming down from the mountains! We're starting just a trickle, but soon we'll be a branch. And the branches will run together to form a little river, and the little rivers will come together to form a great and mighty river, and we'll be swelling and rushing together toward the sea!"

I'd been hanging around the snake handlers long enough by then to know that Brother Bob Stanley was talking about a South that resided in the blood, a region of the heart. Listen up. The peculiarity of Southern experience didn't end when the boll weevil ate up the cotton crop. We didn't cease to be a separate country when Burger King came to Meridian. We're as peculiar a people now as we ever were, and the fact that our culture is under assault has forced us to become even more peculiar than we were before. Snake handling, for instance, didn't originate back in the hills somewhere. It

started when people came *down* from the hills to discover
they were surrounded by a hostile and spiritually dead culture. All along their border with the modern world — in
places like Newport, Tennessee, and Sand Mountain,
Alabama — they recoiled. They threw up defenses. When
their own resources failed, they called down the Holy Ghost.
They put their hands through fire. They drank poison. They
took up serpents.

They still do. The South hasn't disappeared. If anything,
it's become more Southern in a last-ditch effort to save itself.
And the South that survives will last longer than the one that
preceded it. It'll be harder and more durable than what came
before. Why? It's been through the fire. And I'm not just
talking about the civil rights movement, although certainly
that's a place we could start. I'm talking about the long,
slow-burning fire, the original civil war and the industrialization that it spawned. I'm talking about the colonization of
the South by northern entrepreneurs. I'm talking about the
migration to the cities, the cholera epidemics, the floods. I'm
talking about the wars that Southerners fought dispropor-
tionately in this century, the poverty they endured. I'm talking about our fall from Grace. I'm talking about the scorn
and ridicule the nation has heaped on poor Southern whites,
the only ethnic group in America not permitted to have a
history. I'm talking about the City. I don't mean Atlanta. I
mean Birmingham.

In the country, they put their evil spirits in colored glass bottles hung on trees. But let me tell you what we do with evil spirits in the City. We start with coal that a bunch of our male ancestors died getting out of the ground. We heat it in ovens till it gives off poisonous gases and turns into coke, something harder and blacker than it was to begin with. Then we set that coke on fire. We use it to fuel our furnaces. These furnaces are immense things, bulb shaped and covered with rust. You wouldn't want one in your neighborhood. We fill the furnace with limestone and iron ore and any evil spirits we find lying around. The iron ore melts in the coke-driven fire. Impurities attach to the limestone and float to the top. What settles to the bottom is pure and incredibly hot. At a precise moment, we open a hole in the bottom of the furnace, and molten iron cascades out, a ribbon of red so bright you can hardly look at it. When I was a kid you could stand on the viaduct above the Sloss furnaces in downtown Birmingham and watch the river of molten iron racing along the ground, incandescent, inexorable, and so unpredictable that a spark from it flew up one night while my father's friend, Ross Keener, was leaning over the rail of the viaduct, flew up and put out his eye.

That's the kind of South I'm talking about.

1
FOLLOWING SIGNS

One night in East Tennessee, a snake-handling preacher came up to us and said, "You boys got any snakes in that car?"

We told him we didn't.

"What? You mean to tell me you don't have any rattlesnakes in your car?"

"No, sir."

His eyes widened. "What's the matter with you boys?" he said. "Are you crazy?"

The first time I went to a snake-handling service, nobody even took a snake out. This was in Scottsboro, Alabama, in March of 1992, at The Church of Jesus with Signs Following. I'd come to the church at the invitation of one of the members I'd met while covering the trial of their preacher, Rev. Glenn Summerford, who had been convicted and sentenced to ninety-nine years in prison for attempting to murder his wife with rattlesnakes.

The church was on a narrow blacktop called Woods Cove Road, not far from the Jackson County Hospital. I remember it was a cool evening. The sky was the color of apricots, and the moon had just risen, a thin, silver crescent. There weren't any stars out yet.

After I crossed a set of railroad tracks past the hospital, I could see the lights of the church in the distance, but as I drew nearer I started to wonder if this were really a church at all. It was, in fact, a converted gas station and country store, with a fiberboard façade and a miniature steeple. The hand-painted sign spelled the preacher's first name in three different ways: Glenn, Glen, and Glyn. A half dozen cars were parked out front, and even with the windows of my own car rolled up, I could feel the beat of the music.

That music was like nothing I'd ever heard before, a cross between Salvation Army and acid rock: tambourines, an electric guitar, drums, cymbals, and voices that careened from one note to the next as though the singers were being sawn in half. "*I shall not be . . . I shall not be moved. I shall not be . . . I shall not be moved. Just like a tree that's planted by the wa-a-ter, oh . . . I shall not be moved!*"

There are moments when you stand on the brink of a new experience and understand that you have no choice about it. Either you walk into the experience or you turn away from it, but you know that no matter what you choose, you will have altered your life in a permanent way. Either way, there will be consequences.

I walked on in.

A dozen or so men and women were clapping hands and stomping feet. They had the angular, hand-me-down look of Appalachian hill people, and some of them were familiar to me from the trial. I recognized the bald head and wispy, white beard of Uncle Ully Lynn, whom I'd talked to in the witness room during a recess. He seemed to be dressed in the same faded overalls, and his pale blue eyes were as serene and mysterious as they had been at the trial.

"What's it like to take up a serpent?" I had asked him then.

"It's hard to explain," Uncle Ully had said. "You're in a prayerful state. You can't have your mind on other things. The Spirit tells you what to do."

"But why do some people get bit?"

He thought about it a minute. "In that situation," he said, "somebody must have misjudged the Spirit."

In his youth, the story went, Uncle Ully had been one of the biggest gospel singers on Sand Mountain, but I didn't know that then. I also didn't know that within a year he'd be dead, eaten from the inside out by a gangrenous infection that had nothing to do with snakes. At the time of his death, Uncle Ully was still receiving royalties for the songs he'd written for his relative, Loretta Lynn, but that story, too, was one I wouldn't hear till he was gone. All I knew on that first night was that Uncle Ully was a snake handler who seemed to have been a good enough judge of the Spirit to stay alive when others hadn't.

Beyond Uncle Ully's bobbing bald head, I could make out Sister Bobbie Sue Thompson, the woman who had first invited me to the service. She smiled and motioned for me to join her at the front of the church, where she appeared to be leading the singing. At her side stood a woman in a snake-skin-print shirt. I didn't know the words to the songs, but that didn't seem to matter. We sang mostly choruses — "I Saw the Light," "Wading through Deep Water," and "Will the Circle Be Unbroken." The guitar player, a redheaded gnome of a man named Cecil, played surprisingly well. Standing beside him, I was able to get a good look at the church.

Before Glenn Summerford's trial, attendance at The Church of Jesus with Signs Following had reportedly neared a hundred people on any of the three nights during the week when services were held. How all those people fit into the tiny sanctuary was a mystery. The church didn't have more than a dozen pews, and its linoleum floor buckled like a cresting wave. The white walls were bare except for portraits of Jesus and a faded tapestry of the Last Supper. An electric heater glowed in the middle of the room. There were bathrooms off a hall in back.

When the singing wound down, a short, wiry man with a mustache and slicked-back hair headed for the pulpit. He was carrying a Bible in one hand and a flat wooden serpent box in the other. He wore a dark, western-style shirt, jeans, and a Jesus belt buckle. The portrait of Jesus on the buckle was not one of those conventional ones in which the Lord appears to be a mild-mannered aesthete with shampooed hair. This man's Jesus was more like the wild-eyed Jewish carpenter who had chased the money changers from the temple.

"I ain't no preacher," the man said apologetically. His bottom front teeth were missing. I'd later find out his name was J.L. "I ain't no assistant preacher either," he said. "I'm just trying to keep the church open."

"Amen," Sister Bobbie Sue said.

J.L. gingerly set the snake box on the altar, and there was an awkward silence as he lay his Bible on the pulpit and slowly thumbed through it. His fingers were square and his nails dark — workman's hands. He was a welder with a bad heart who dreamed of artificially inseminating his own cattle, I later learned.

"Help him, Jesus," Sister Bobbie Sue said.

"The text is gonna be John 3:16," J.L. finally said. He read haltingly, one finger in the book, his dark eyebrows knit. An odd thing about the place occurred to me even then. When it's absolutely still and quiet in a church like The Church of Jesus with Signs Following, even then there's an impression of movement, as though a light were swinging from a chain, but there wasn't any such light that night. It was an illusion, I thought. Something there that wasn't.

"*For God so loved the world,*" J.L. read, "*that he gave his only begotten Son, that whosoever believeth in him should not perish, but have everlasting life.*"

"Amen," said Sister Bobbie Sue.

"Bless His sweet name," said the woman in the snakeskin shirt.

J.L. looked up, considering his next words. "God *so* loved the world," he said. And then: "Let us pray."

It had to have been the shortest sermon in history. But nobody seemed to mind. They all came to the front, the women in their ankle-length dresses with the lace collars and tiny flowered prints, the men in their jeans, overalls, or polyester slacks. They knelt at the makeshift altar and started praying out loud, each a different prayer. J.L.'s voice rose above the others for a measure or so. "O Lord, be with us now, and in thy mercy hold and keep us, and O Dear God, bless this our little church, amen, and keep it for your own. . . ."

Then another voice rose up to meet his, entered into fellowship with it, and fell away, each voice on a separate strand of meaning but weaving with the others into a kind of song, rising and falling, gathering and dispersing, and high above it all like a descant ran the voice of Glenn Summerford's mother, Aunt Annie Mance. She was praying for her son, in prison for ninety-nine years for a crime she said he couldn't have committed, and her voice joined in a duet with another woman's plea for her own lost children, living in the city, in sin, and just beneath the women were

Uncle Ully's raspy, grasshopper voice and Sister Bobbie Sue's bluesy one. And underneath all the human voices was the incessant rattle of the serpent in the wooden box.

No one called for the prayer to end. The voices simply fell into a shared rhythm that gradually tapered off, subsiding in volume and in pitch. The sounds of the rattlesnake remained constant while the voices disassembled themselves, but finally even the snake went silent, and the prayer concluded with amens that fell on top of one another like the half-sighed endings of a round.

I stepped outside after my first service at The Church of Jesus with Signs Following and wondered where the time had gone. It was nearly ten o'clock. That crescent of moon had disappeared behind Sand Mountain. The stars, bright as ice, had popped out.

Some of the men were gathered in the parking lot. They were talking about how it used to be before Glenn's arrest, when the church was filled with families from all over Jackson County. "They'll be back," said Cecil, the guitar player, and he patted me on the arm. "You come back, too."

I grew up in a Methodist church, but ours must have been an odd kind of Methodism. We were a small congregation in East Lake, an urban residential neighborhood of Birmingham, and occasionally we'd get a preacher from what we thought of as the sticks, from a place like East Gadsden, a small mill town at the foot of the Appalachians, or Arab, pronounced A-rab, on the top of Brindley Mountain.

These preachers sometimes seemed a little out of place in our quiet, sober neighborhood, where the families of grocers and plumbers and office workers tried to secure a hold on middle-class respectability. The preachers would attempt to liven up the services by shouting till they were hoarse. Sometimes they resorted to bolder tactics. In the middle of a sermon, for instance, Brother Jack Dillard, my favorite, would suddenly be so overcome by the Spirit, he would run down to the piano and start banging away on it. He could not, in fact, play the piano, but that didn't seem to matter.

Brother Dillard believed in obeying the Spirit, and he encouraged those grocers and tradesmen to do the same, although I don't recall ever seeing any of them follow his example. Of course, all of us teenagers got saved in that church during Brother Dillard's tenure, some of us multiple times. The record was held by a girl named Frances Fuller, who never passed up an opportunity to rush to the altar. She occasionally had a seizure halfway there, and someone would have to run to the kitchen to find a spoon to put in her mouth. The choir would continue to sing "All to Jesus I Surrender," and I remember my father's grip would tighten on the back of the pew in front of him until they got Frances up on her feet and back in her seat again.

What we really worried about, though, was Brother Dillard's heart. Years later, it would kill him. We worried because he always worked himself into such a sweat when he preached that he would have to take out his handkerchief and mop his forehead, cheeks, and neck. This was such a familiar habit that it didn't distract us one bit from his sermon, not even the Sunday when, instead of pulling his handkerchief out, he retrieved his pocket comb by mistake and began combing his hair while he shouted, "When we were yet sinners, He died for us!"

Those days were filled with desperate innocence and with a spiritual light that I would later miss. We were a naive little church, always prey to a good sob story — the missionary we sponsored in what was then Southern Rhodesia, for instance. Years later we discovered he actually owned a fairly sizable rubber plantation, on which local villagers worked for next to nothing. The young men lived in barracks on the plantation, and the owner would have informal Bible study with them sometimes at night. For this, he was called a missionary, and we would send him a good portion of our foreign missions budget every month.

And then there was Dr. Doctorin. Dr. Doctorin came to us in 1958, at a time when the newspapers were filled with stories about Lebanon's civil war, and with photographs of U.S. Marines wading ashore in Beirut. There was a lot of concern both for our soldiers and for the poor Lebanese. We considered ourselves fortunate when Dr. Doctorin showed up at our church one Sunday night to conduct an impromptu revival. The timing could not have been better. Dr. Doctorin said that he had just come from Beirut. We took up a huge love offering for him. I remember that he wept when we brought him the overflowing collection plates.

It was the last time we ever saw Dr. Doctorin, and it was not until many years later that I began to wonder if he really had been a doctor, and if his name could really have been Dr. Doctorin, and if he were really from Beirut.

We weren't always right in our assessment of people and their intentions, but we had a simple, childlike faith, something Jesus said he approved of. And if my experience in that church did nothing else for me, it accustomed me to strange outpourings of the Spirit and gave me a tender regard for con artists and voices in the wilderness, no matter how odd or suspicious their message might be. I believe it also put me in touch with a rough-cut and reckless side of myself that I otherwise might never have recognized, locked way back somewhere in cell memory, a cultural legacy I would have otherwise known nothing about. You see, growing up in East Lake, where people were trying so hard to escape their humble pasts, I had come of age not knowing much about my family history. As far as we were concerned, the Covingtons went back only two generations, to our grandparents. My grandfather on my mother's side had been a railroad detective and had died of syphilis. My father's father had also ridden the trains, as a postal clerk. Later in life, I would discover that Covingtons had not always lived in Birmingham, but that at some point we, too, had come down from the mountains, and that those wild-eyed, perspiring preachers of my childhood were kin to me in a way I could never have expected or fully appreciated. In retrospect, I believe that my religious education had pointed me all along toward some ultimate rendezvous with people who took up serpents.

Even without the snakes, my first trip to a snake-handling church had been exhilarating and unsettling. I drove back to Birmingham that night in a heightened and confused state, as though the pupils of my spiritual eyes had been dilated. The sensation was uncomfortable but not entirely unpleasant. Whatever this was about, I wanted to experience more. And of course I *had* to see what they did with the snakes.

It was the very next night, on my second trip to The Church of Jesus with Signs Following, that the snakes came out. Brother Carl Porter had driven from his home church in Kingston, Georgia, to deliver the message. A retired truck driver whose CB handle had been "Sneaky Snake," Brother Carl looked more like a barber, or someone's favorite uncle.

He was an unassuming man in his late forties, with a nose that was a bit flattened on the end. His eyes were close together, and his hair was thin. Nothing in his demeanor hinted at his peculiar power behind the pulpit. Seeing him on the street, you would never have suspected that the Spirit of God regularly moved upon him, or that he handled rattlesnakes.

But to the congregation of The Church of Jesus with Signs Following, Brother Carl was a special man indeed. Ever since Glenn Summerford's arrest, he had been driving over when he could to fill in for Glenn. It was clearly an uncomfortable position for him to be in, now that Glenn had been convicted, but Brother Carl must have seen his duties as a kind of mission.

On this night, Brother Carl was accompanied by his wife, Carolyn, and some other members of their church in Kingston, including Aunt Daisy Parker, a severe-looking old woman with an unpredictable temperament. The singing and praying had gone on for about an hour when Aunt Daisy suddenly leapt to her feet and began to prophesy.

"There's gonna come a day," she said, "when the bellies of the earth will open up, and some'll be set free and some'll be devoured!"

Then she started marching. Daisy's white hair was tied in a bun at the back of her head. She was skinny and hunched a bit at the shoulders, and she swung her arms in the air as she marched. "And oh Lord, on that day, there's gonna be some that'll be taken out of that prison and put back in the heart of God where they belong!"

The rest of the congregation amened. "Oh, the earth is gonna shake!" she said. "It'll tear the chains from the wall that are holding him. And the sky will turn as red as blood. They'll be smoke and confusion everywheres when God sends his dark messenger to roll over the rooftops and loose the prisoner from his sleep!"

I was sitting in the middle of the congregation and watching Aunt Daisy with increasing alarm. I hoped she wouldn't get the urge to march in my direction. In any other context, I would have pegged her as an obvious lunatic. But then I realized that the rest of the congregation seemed not only to indulge her but to understand her. She was prophesying Glenn Summerford's miraculous escape from prison, and at about that time, the revelation seemed to sweep over the congregation all at once. Glenn's mother burst into tears.

"And there's nothing the world can do to prevent it!" Daisy said. "The world will have no power against it!" She was standing at the front of the church now, and she pointed her finger into the center of the congregation at some unnamed and unseen adversary. "They'll have no power against it!"

With that, she swooned and collapsed onto the front pew.
Amen! That's when Brother Carl stood up to preach. He had
one hand in his pocket, and he smiled down at Aunt Daisy
as she roused herself to a sitting position on the pew. I
would later find out that Brother Carl was like a son to her,
and that he took her prophecies dead seriously. At the time,
though, I thought he was trying to distance himself from her
outburst.

"It's hot in here, ain't it?" he said. Everybody laughed.
They knew he wasn't talking about the temperature, but I
thought that he was. I also thought that Carl Porter was a
man for whom preaching could not have been a natural or
comfortable talent. He had made his way to the pulpit tenta-
tively, like a badger who has just ventured out of his burrow
and isn't entirely easy with what he sees. He wore a rumpled
white dress shirt, open at the collar, and polyester slacks. His
glasses had slipped to the end of his nose. In the future I'd
see a more flamboyant side, but on this night, he was dressed
unobtrusively and started out his sermon as though the Lord
didn't have anything particular for him to say. Then he
opened up his Bible.

"Let's look over here in the second chapter of Acts," he
said. *"And when the day of Pentecost was fully come, they
were all with one accord in one place. And suddenly there
came a sound from heaven as of a rushing mighty wind, and*

it filled all the house where they were sitting. And there appeared unto them cloven tongues like as of fire, and it sat upon each of them. And they were all filled with the Holy Ghost, and began to speak with other tongues, as the Spirit gave them utterance."

He closed his Bible, looked at it a second, picked it up, looked at it some more, and said, "The Holy Ghost wouldn't come until they was all of one accord." Then he looked at us. "That's what the Word says, and honey, the Word says what it means and it means what it says."

There was a chorus of amens from the congregation, and Cecil, the guitar player, ran his finger up the frets with a *scree*.

"They was gathered together of one accord," Brother Carl continued, "and you know, this book wasn't just written for the apostles. This wasn't just something that happened to the apostles. When the Holy Ghost came down with tongues of fire and they started speaking in the unknown tongue, God didn't intend for just the apostles to do that."

And here he grimaced, as though he had stepped on something sharp. He ducked to one side of the pulpit and came up bobbing. "Jesus sent the Holy Ghost for us," he said and slapped the pulpit with the flat of his hand. "You know, some people are still sitting around waiting for the Holy Ghost to come. It already came, at Pentecost! And it's been coming ever since! I can feel it all over me right now," he said. "Whoo!" And he did a little hopping dance on one foot while Cecil plucked the guitar strings in accompaniment. "Whoo! It just goes from my feet all the way to my head. I just love it when it gets in my hair," he said.

He came out fully from behind the pulpit, the Bible outstretched in one hand. "Honey, that Holy Ghost is here right now for me and you. But let me tell you, we better be of one accord if we want the Holy Ghost to move on us, because the Holy Ghost ain't gonna move on a bunch of people that aren't of one accord." *Amen. Thank God.* "This God we worship, he's a living God." *Amen.* "God ain't no white-bearded old man up in the sky somewhere. He's a spirit." *Amen. Thank God.* "He's a spirit. He ain't got no body." *Amen. Thank God.* "The only body he's got is us." *Amen. Thank God.* "And when we're borned again, we're borned into the body of God!"

Most of the congregation were standing by now, clapping and stomping their feet. Brother Carl took out a handkerchief and wiped his forehead. Then he took off his glasses and began cleaning them with it. "Whew!" he said when the ruckus had died down. "I'm glad I'm His, aren't you?" *Amen. Thank God.* "And I'm glad He's mine, aren't you? I wouldn't have it any other way. I wouldn't have no other God. No, sir. I want the *real* thing. And let me tell you, this thing is real." He folded up his glasses and put them back in his breast pocket. "I don't guess you heard me. I said, this thing is real!"

Those that weren't already standing sprang to their feet, hands stretched up, amening and praising God.

Brother Carl opened his Bible again, but he didn't need to refer to it this time. "It was after they crucified Him," he said, "and the women came to the grave. They didn't find Him there, did they? He was plumb gone out of there. But a man dressed in white said He'd risen and would appear to them later, and He did. And you know what He said, don't you?"

Amen. They all knew what He had said.

"He said, *And these signs shall follow them that believe; In my name shall they cast out devils; they shall speak with new tongues; They shall take up serpents; and if they drink any deadly thing, it shall not hurt them; they shall lay hands on the sick, and they shall recover!*"

A sawmill worker named Willie Southard was walking up and down the aisle, clapping his hands like a metronome and praising the name of Jesus.

"After that," Brother Carl said, "Jesus went up to heaven, where he sat on the right hand of God. And you know what it says about them believers, don't you? It says, *They went forth, and preached every where, the Lord working with them, and confirming the word with signs following. Amen!*"

He lay his Bible on the pulpit in triumph. He took a hard look at the wooden serpent box that rested on the bench that served as an altar. It was a flat, finely joined box stained the color of coffee. The top was hinged, half screen and half wood, and the corners were reinforced with decorative studs. Brother Carl leaned over and tapped at the screen. The dry rattling that arose from the box seemed to satisfy him. I figured that's when he would take up a serpent, but he didn't. He hopped around a little more while Cecil improvised on guitar. Then Brother Carl did a stutter step and seemed to stumble, catching himself at the last minute. He shuddered. He shook. He praised and shouted and prayed. Cecil finally launched into a full-blown song that the congregation started singing, and then another.

We were singing "Prayer Bells from Heaven" when Brother Carl finally opened the hinged door of the wooden box and lifted out a canebrake rattlesnake. It was fat and desultory, a yellowish gray. After holding it up to the light, he passed it to Willie Southard and took out a copperhead that had almost finished shedding its skin.

The copperhead was bronze and gold in the overhead light. Brother Carl held it up, regarding it with something like suspicion and regret. The snake tested the air with its tongue. Brother Carl put his thumb in front of the snake's head, letting the snake touch it with its tongue. Then he put his face up to the snake's face. They seemed to watch each other for a moment, until the snake drew back and began searching the air again with its tongue. Brother Carl let the snake fall to his side and then lifted it up again. This time he held the snake high above his head, part draped over his forearm, the rest stretched across the tips of his fingers. It was as though he were holding aloft a fine gold chain, some elegant piece of filigree. When the snake slowly moved in and out of Brother Carl's fingers, bits of shed skin fell to the floor. The snake appeared to be in the process of reinventing itself, forging a new self out of the old.

After a few minutes, Brother Carl put the snakes back into the box. The service went on for another half hour. He and Uncle Ully anointed Glenn Summerford's mother with oil, and she testified that it felt like electricity running up and down her arms. Sister Bobbie Sue led us in another round of songs. Aunt Daisy spoke in tongues. But it was the image of that newly shed copperhead that I couldn't shake as I stepped into the dark night outside the church. Why had I been drawn to it? What did it mean? The air was frigid. It had been a late, cold spring, and by morning the branches of the flowering peach would be encased in ice.

I heard Brother Carl behind me before I turned and saw him silhouetted in the yellow light from the open door of the church. He stepped out into the parking lot. "I hear you're a writer," he said and shook my hand.

I nodded and apologized for taking notes during the service.

"What are you writing about?" he asked.

I told him I'd covered Glenn Summerford's trial and that I was writing a book about snake handling.

He glanced away as if he'd heard that one before. "The Bible says Jesus won't come again until the gospel's been published in every nation," he said. "So you just go ahead and write that book. As long as you tell the truth, it'll be edifying to the body of Christ. It'll be like you're spreading the gospel, won't it?"

I nodded. But I wondered if Brother Carl knew then about the inevitable treachery that stood between journalist and subject. I wondered if he was ready for the dance that would have to take place between him and me.

2
THE TRIAL

———

Scottsboro, Alabama, is Southern, but not in the way you'd expect. It doesn't have a cotton gin in ruins by the railroad tracks or a dusty avenue lined with magnolia trees and Greek revival homes. Instead, it's an efficient little mill town at the foot of the Appalachians in the northeast corner of the state, a stone's throw away from the Tennessee River. Scottsboro has wide, clean streets, a thriving commercial district, and a no-nonsense county courthouse, square lined and unadorned, rebuilt after the war, and I don't mean the Civil War. I mean World War II.

Sixty years ago, though, the old courthouse on that same site was the scene of a sensational trial that put Scottsboro on the map and forever linked its name with the failed plantation culture nearly two hundred miles to the south. Nine black youths, who came to be called the Scottsboro Boys, were convicted of the rape of two white women, a verdict later overturned by the United States Supreme Court.

The memory of that trial is a burden residents of Scottsboro say they could do without. They point out with some heat that the Scottsboro Boys were not from Scottsboro at all, but were simply riding through on a freight train. The alleged crime, the trial, and the attendant nationwide publicity were accidents of history, they say, that have marked the town unjustly for life.

Residents would prefer to talk about Scottsboro's present — its composed and photogenic town square; its famous First Monday Trade Days, one of the oldest craft shows and flea markets in the South; and the new Bellefonte nuclear power plant, which is drawing physicists, engineers, and other professional people to the area. Scottsboro, residents say, has a lot to offer these new immigrants. The fishing is great in the sloughs of Lake Guntersville, the town's strip boasts a Chinese restaurant and a trendy sports bar, and golf and sailing are de rigueur at Goose Pond Colony, a 360-acre resort and recreation complex just south of the city limits.

But to even the casual observer, there's a third Scottsboro, a town quite different from the one fixed in history or the one portrayed in the contemporary chamber of commerce brochures. Its emblem could have been that converted store and filling station out on Woods Cove Road, the one with the miniature steeple and the sign out front that read "The Church of Jesus with Signs Following."

This was the Scottsboro of Rev. Glenn Summerford and his flock, many of whose families had come down from the mountains after World War II and had been trying to eke out a living and a sense of dignity ever since. Some had come from Tater Knob to the north of town or Poorhouse Mountain to the west. But most had come from Sand Mountain to the east, an enormous plateau twenty-five miles across and seventy-five miles long, one of the southernmost reaches of the Appalachians and an island of possibility in the midst of a Southern culture in crisis.

In northeastern Alabama, as in much of the rest of the South, progress since World War II has been double-edged: it has meant higher wages, better health, and less isolation from the rest of the world, but it has also meant the loss of a traditional way of life. The hill people had prided themselves on their independence and self-sufficiency. They grew what they ate, bartered for what they couldn't grow, and did without those conveniences they couldn't fashion out of the materials at hand. But contact with the dominant culture in the cities and towns began to change all that. The new highways, increased personal income, and better communication led to rising expectations and a migration away from areas like rural northeastern Alabama toward the magnets of Nashville, Chattanooga, and Birmingham. Families were torn apart and separated from the land. Language and habits of mind began to be lost, as were old arts like divining water, snaking logs, and killing hogs. People stopped saying "I'll swan" for "I'll swear," as their ancestors had done in North Britain for centuries. And the dead were no longer laid out with platters of salt on their stomachs, a ritual once meant to evoke the immortality of the soul.

Today, Sand Mountain's crossroad towns boast new libraries and civic centers, but the countryside itself is littered with burned-out house trailers, automobile graveyards, collapsed chicken farms, and those ubiquitous totems of cultural anomie — tanning beds and late-night video stores. Marijuana is a major cash crop on the mountain. Illegal cockfighting appears to be a favorite pastime. "Sand Mountain is a law unto itself," says one federal drug enforcement official. The lure of the secular and worldly in a region once characterized as the Bible Belt has left a residue of rootlessness, anxiety, and lawlessness.

Enter the snake handlers, spiritual nomads from the high country that surrounded Scottsboro, from isolated pockets on Sand Mountain and the hollows along South Sauty Creek. They were refugees from a culture on the ropes. They spoke in tongues, anointed one another with oil in order to be healed, and when instructed by the Holy Ghost, drank poison, held fire, and took up poisonous snakes. For them, Scottsboro itself was the wicked, wider world, a place where one might be tempted to "back up on the Lord." They'd taken the risk, though, out of economic desperation. They had been drawn to Scottsboro by the promise of jobs in the mills that made clothes, carpets, rugs, and tires. Some of them had found work. All of them had found prejudice.

"They call us 'Old Jesus Onlys,' 'freaks,' and 'Holy Rollers,'" said Sister Bobbie Sue Thompson, one of Glenn Summerford's most ardent supporters at his trial. But she'd learned to live with the ridicule. It was part of the price, she said, that believers paid for being what the Bible calls "a separated people" who were "*in* the world, but not *of* the world."

When the handlers came down to Scottsboro, they began meeting in houses along Tupelo Pike. Their first church in town burned to the ground. They suspected arson, but charges were never brought. They felt like they'd gotten the message, though. So they moved to other locations, some clandestine, some not. For a while they had a place above Five Points and one down at Mink Creek. When they met above a restaurant called the Chicken Basket, their neighbors complained of the noise. Wherever the handlers relocated, tires got slashed and windows broken, even after they moved to the converted filling station out on Woods Cove Road. But there, the handlers felt they had found a permanent home. It was on a quiet stretch of road beyond the railroad

tracks, its only neighbor an auto repair shop and weed-
choked junkyard. The congregation didn't draw as much
hostile attention there as they had in town. And they could
turn their electric guitars up as loud as they wanted.

During services at the church, the congregation worshiped
in typical Holiness fashion, except for their peculiar embell-
ishments. Glenn Summerford, a small-time hoodlum who had
repented and been called to preach, routinely handled poisonous snakes, drank strychnine, and stuck his fingers into live
electrical sockets. But what created a sensation in Scottsboro
in the fall of 1991 was his arrest on charges that he had used
rattlesnakes, that symbol of faith to him and his followers, in
an attempt to murder his wife.

Glenn Summerford's arrest merited only a brief notice in one
of the Birmingham newspapers, but I read about it with
interest. I had just started stringing for *The New York Times*
and was on the lookout for out-of-the-way places in the
news that might serve as settings for what the national desk
called "journal" pieces. I'd never been to Scottsboro, but I'd
heard of the Scottsboro Boys. My editor liked the story idea,
so I hit the road. I had no idea what lay in store.

Travel was ideal, a bright winter morning, and I was
bowled over by the mountains and lakes south of Scottsboro,
the wood ducks and Canada geese. Once there, I had no trou-

ble finding the renovated brick courthouse with its original white cupola intact. Satellite news trucks from Chattanooga and Huntsville were parked outside the courthouse, and print journalists and curiosity seekers unable to get into the courtroom loitered around in the halls, which smelled of stale urine and cigarette smoke.

The trial was in its second day. Jury selection had been completed, opening arguments made, and the state's star witness, Darlene Summerford, had begun her initial testimony in a second-floor courtroom packed with hard, angular women and men with slicked-back hair and unfortunate teeth. Many of the details of Darlene Summerford's story fell together over the course of the trial, as well as from conversations I had with her afterward.

The story begins in a ghost town in the shadow of the twin cooling towers of the Bellefonte nuclear power plant, which hasn't yet gone on-line. It's a humid evening, the first week of October, with a moon as thin as a woman's fingernail. The wind has picked up. An empty Coke cup skitters across the rotted porch of the town's abandoned hotel. The cup is followed by a whirl of curled poplar leaves, which gradually disperse and fall to earth. And then the air is still and silent, except for the singing of the last frogs and the rumble of eighteen-wheelers out on highway 72.

Through the trees on the river side of town, a barge filled with lumber makes its way down the Tennessee River, shedding a cone of light over the water. As the barge enters a bend, the light touches the banks on either side and the overgrown streets of the abandoned town. On the highway on the other side of town, the twin headlights of a car flicker through the trees. One of the headlights is askew, spewing its light into the branches, and the car, a Chevy Chevette with Alabama tags, is going dangerously fast.

"I oughta throw you in the river," the driver says. He is a powerfully built man with graying hair slicked into a pompadour, and he shifts in his seat as though he were a kind of animal and the car a kind of cage. The woman in the passenger's seat, Darlene Summerford, is staring straight ahead. She has long, thick auburn hair and the lean, kept look of Southern Appalachian women. Like them she has been used to the bone and is nursing a hurt, in this case a swollen and blackened thumb that she holds in her lap. "I shoulda throwed you in the sinkhole up at Woodville," the man continues.

"Slow down," she says. "I'm getting sick again."

"Good." He glares at her. "Maybe you're finally starting to die."

"You wish, don't you."

"I could wish for worse."

"So you could go visit your whore every day," she spits.

"Who's calling who a whore?" he says.

"I'm too sick to argue," she says. "You said you'd take me to the hospital if I went to Paint Rock with you."

"That was yesterday I said that."

"I know. And now it's today. We been to Paint Rock, we been to the liquor store, we been to the video store, but I haven't seen no hospital yet."

"And you're not going to see one if I can help it."

For the first time since they got in the car, Darlene looks over at her husband. Even after everything he's done, she's still shocked at the way he has deceived her into helping him set up his alibi. A preacher with the unlikely name of Glendel Buford Summerford, he goes by Glenn, but not even she is sure whether his first name's got one *n* or two. Married as long as they've been, long enough to have a thirteen-year-old son, you'd think she would know that for sure, but it's just one of many things about him she's never figured out. She still thinks of his face as familiar, despite the web-like intricacies of light over it now, handiwork of the venom in her brain. She's already been bit by one of his rattlesnakes, and she knows if she were to look too closely at the threads of light, she'd see living things marching along them, convoys of geometric insects multiplying right before her eyes, so she doesn't let her eyes focus on anything but the gap in Glenn's teeth, which even though she hates him, is a reminder that she at least knows who he is.

This isn't the first time she's been bit. The first time was when she fell in love with him. And then there was that time when she thought the Holy Ghost was moving on her, but she must have read the Spirit wrong, because the rattler got her on the chest, just below her collarbone, right during a chorus of "I Saw the Light." But last night was different; last night was the first time the handling wasn't her idea, the first time it wasn't in church. It was in the shed behind their house on Barbee Lane. That's where Glenn kept the snakes, all seventeen of them, in a series of wooden cages and two old aquariums tied together with baling wire. Glenn had been in a drunken, jealous rage for days. He'd accused her of cheating on him. He'd knocked her around, pulled her hair. Finally, he had put a gun to her head and forced her to stick her hand into one of the cages, and then later, after the diamondback rattlesnake had bit her and she'd stumbled on the way back to the house and fallen to the ground, he unzipped his fly and pissed on her. That was how bad it had got. He'd made her get bit by a snake and then pissed on her, and now he was driving ninety to nothing down highway 72, threatening to throw her into a sinkhole or into the river. He was drunker than Cooter Brown. "You've *got* to die," he'd been telling her. Good Lord, how'd things get this way? She had tried all

day to think things through. It is the first time Glenn has
ever *seriously* tried to kill her. And as he slows to make the
turn off the highway and away from Scottsboro proper and
the Jackson County hospital, it occurs to her that he will
succeed on his first try.

The lights of the car flash against the Sisks' house, and
Darlene wishes that Walter and Eva Ruth would look out
their window and see her and know how terribly wrong
things are. She knows they love her. They always have something kind to say to her when she goes to the door to pay the
twenty-five-dollar rent, which Mr. Sisk turns over to Mr.
Tipton, the lawyer who owns the property. She imagines the
way Eva Ruth's face will collapse when she learns that
Darlene Summerford has died at her husband's hands. The
car passes the Cunningham place and the Chambless place
and then bumps up Barbee Lane through fields of dried soy-
beans and morning glories that seem to spring up, purple
and pink, in the headlights. Glenn slows enough to negotiate
the drainage ditch between the posts of the electric fence,
past the pony shed and the dog pen, and when he finally
brings the car to a stop next to the familiar house with the
tin roof and brown asphalt siding, Darlene shudders with
the understanding that she is home.

She wants to stay in the car, but Glenn motions her out of
the car and toward the house. Inside, he makes her sit at the

kitchen table and places a pen and a loose-leaf binder in front of her. Then he puts the gun to her head and tells her to write down exactly what he's fixing to say. The room is spinning. She can hardly see the page, but he nudges the barrel of the pistol against her ear, and she starts to write when he starts to speak. It takes her a minute to figure out what he's doing. Then it hits her. He's making her write a suicide note to their son, Marty, who's been staying with one of Glenn's daughters since the latest fight began: "Marty, I love you. Do what Daddy says. Daddy was asleep. I tried to fix things but it didn't work out. Daddy's asleep. He don't know what I'm doing. I went out and got snake bit. Glenn is asleep. I don't want no help." She begs him to let her stop writing. She's going to throw up. She leans away from the table, but nothing comes up now but bile. He makes her keep on writing. He's so drunk he has trouble stringing the words together, and he keeps repeating himself. "Daddy was asleep. Daddy's asleep. Glenn is asleep." She writes it all.

Then he orders her outside, back to the shed, and this time he forces her to stick her hand into the cage with the big canebrake. He grabs her hair and twists it around his hand until it feels like her scalp is going to be pulled away from her skull. She's got a choice, he tells her. Either she sticks her hand in on her own, or he'll press her face into the cage, and she can take the bite on her cheek or in her eye. "Pray and get things right with God," he says, "'cause this time you're gonna die." She chooses to stick her left hand in, the same one that got bit the night before, and the canebrake rises and bites her on the back of it. This time the nausea seems to hit her even before the pain. She retches into the dirt. Glenn shoves her toward the house. She stumbles and falls. He kicks her. He pulls her up by the hair. When she staggers to her feet, he shoves her again toward the back door.

In the kitchen, he pours himself another vodka and orange juice and waves her to the living room. She remembers to duck so she won't hit her head on the doorframe. And in the living room she collapses into an overstuffed chair. The pain is unbearable now. She's drifting in and out of a vivid, night-mare sleep. One minute she's watching the convoys of insects on the highways at the back of her mind's eye, the next minute her real eyes are open, the TV's on, all static and a noise like rattlesnakes, and the minute after that she rouses herself enough to see that Glenn has passed out on the couch, his last drink spilled on the floor, the gun still within reach.

Darlene struggles to come fully awake. She waits without moving, alert as radar. He's dead passed out. She knows by the sounds he makes. She gets out of the chair, careful so as not to let the springs creak. Standing up, she almost passes out herself, but she's driven now by something deep and primal. She finds the telephone and takes it into the kitchen. She calls one of her sisters, but keeps it short and quiet. "Glenn made me get bit by a snake," she whispers. "He's fallen asleep. Call the ambulance. I'll meet them on the road by the Chambless place. Tell them not to come up here. Tell them not to run their lights or sirens. It'll wake him up."

When she hangs up, she waits to hear if he is stirring. He's not. She makes her way out the back door, praying the dogs won't start barking. Outside, it has become a clear, cold night. The sky is full of stars. She can see this won't be easy. When she told her sister she'd get to the Chambless place, she'd forgotten how hard it is to move after you've been bitten by two rattlesnakes. She tells herself to put one foot in front of the other, and this works as far as the drainage ditch between the electric fence posts. She leans into one of them. She glances back at the house. Then she gathers her strength. In the far distance she can see the lights of the Chambless place and the Cunningham place, and it is toward them she is headed, partway on foot, partway on her knees. She is not sure whether she is going to live or die. All she knows for certain is that she is headed toward the light.

And later, much later, it seems, when the ambulance attendant takes her arm in the middle of the road, it's as though he is escorting her through a door into a bright room where all this can be explained and given a name. He tells her not to be afraid, and they hook her up to a machine and give her oxygen and wash her hand off, the one that was bit. It is such a simple thing for the attendant to do, but she thinks about it on the way to the emergency room, and later that night, when the same ambulance attendant accompanies her to the big university hospital in Birmingham, she is thinking about how nice it was to have her hand washed off like that. Her hand was mostly numb, but she could still feel it a little, a gentle anointing, both warm and cold, like something she'd receive in church, and she realizes she's been trying to get herself clean from one thing or another for as long as she can remember. Maybe this time, it'll be for good.

During the recess after Darlene's testimony, I found a seat near the front of the courtroom on a pew-like bench reserved for the press.

"I believe they're all cousins," one reporter said as the crowd of onlookers filed back into the courtroom.

The contrast in appearance between us and the people who were attending the trial was striking. Most of the women, no matter their age, wore their hair uncut. It cascaded to the waists of their ankle-length dresses or was pinned atop their heads in gray knots. Few of the women seemed to have on makeup or jewelry, but there were some young rebels with teased hair and dangling earrings, the slogans on their T-shirts years out of style.

The men, with their dark looks and ducktails, were unsettling to me. What might have been nothing more than ordinary decorum in a different social context appeared in this one to be wariness and suspicion. Their glances toward the journalists were thick-lidded and vaguely menacing. But I noticed their expressions did not seem to change even when they were talking with what appeared to be family and friends. It was the same look on the face of Glenn Summerford, who sat at the defense table with his hands in his lap. He was wearing a sky blue shirt, and his eyes seemed far apart and remote. I saw now that the unnerving cast to the men's faces was probably just inflexibility, an unwillingness to give themselves up to public emotion. It had to do not so much with their religion, I reasoned, as with their poverty.

All rose as Judge Loy Campbell entered the courtroom in his motorized wheelchair. He had just read in the news that someone had found Babe Ruth's outhouse, and he passed that information along to the jury before he reconvened the court.

At the prosecutor's table, Darlene Summerford turned to whisper something to the district attorney, Dwight Duke. Darlene was dressed in a white knit dress and hose. She had certainly left her husband's church, but she had not yet cut her auburn hair, and her sullen expression and lupine eyes suggested a wilderness of thought. When she smiled over her shoulder at someone in the courtroom, I wondered what it would be like to be bitten by rattlesnakes. I wondered if there could be any pleasure at all in that, in coming so close to death and surviving. I would find out later that Darlene was four months pregnant, had been pregnant without knowing it when the rattlesnakes bit her, and that the doctors now thought the baby would be fine.

I could hardly take my eyes off Darlene Summerford during the trial, even at the end of the day, when a surprise defense witness took the stand. The prosecution had argued that Glenn had backslid and taken to drink. In a fit of irrational jealousy, he had tried to kill Darlene and disguise it as a suicide. Glenn's attorney, Gary Lackey, had argued that both the Summerfords had backslid and taken to drink, and that the idea for Darlene to stick her hand into the snake cages had been her own.

But the surprise defense witness, Tammy Flippo, twenty-three, said that everybody had it wrong. A birdlike young woman with the distracting habit of twisting the ends of her hair as she talked, Ms. Flippo testified before a hushed courtroom that *Darlene* had been trying to kill *Glenn* with the snake, not the other way around. "She told me she wanted to kill him because she didn't want to live like that no more," Ms. Flippo said. "She was going to let the snake bite Glenn on the neck, but when she reached into the box it bit her instead."

Ms. Flippo's testimony set the courtroom abuzz. "She's lying!" said Ms. Flippo's ex-husband, Ollie T. Ingram, when he cornered me in the hall during a recess.

"In my opinion, she's in love with the minister," added her former sister-in-law, Sylvia Ingram.

After the recess, other witnesses testified that both parties wanted a divorce, but because Darlene feared losing custody of their thirteen-year-old son, and Glenn wanted to keep preaching, divorce was out of the question, and the death of one or the other seemed the only way out.

By the end of the first day of testimony, it was unclear who had tried to kill whom. The only sure thing was that backsliding was serious business in this part of the state.

I stayed in Scottsboro that night, at an economy motel run by a family from India. The room smelled of curry and black-eyed peas, a confusion that mirrored my state of mind. I didn't know who to believe or what the trial was ultimately about. Although the testimony had echoed familiar themes from a troubled secular society — marital infidelity, spousal abuse, and alcoholism — it had also raised questions about faith, forgiveness, redemption, and of course, snakes.

At times, it must have seemed to Darlene that she was on trial instead of Glenn. Glenn's attorney, Gary Lackey, had referred to her as the foremost woman snake handler in the Southeast. He had introduced videos and still photographs of the couple handling snakes, and he had attempted to portray Darlene as a woman with suicidal tendencies and an unhealthy fixation on snakes. Police had found photographs of rattlesnakes in her purse, he reminded the jury.

"Tell me, Mrs. Summerford," he had asked during cross-examination, "did you and your husband ever breed these snakes?"

"Why no, sir," she said. "They did that themselves."

The reporters in the courtroom laughed, and Lackey threw a wry glance at the judge.

I understood why the media attention paid the trial infuriated some of Scottsboro's residents, including the district attorney, Dwight Duke.

"Down the hall," he had said to a room full of reporters, "we've got a trial going on about an eighteen-month-old kid that got beat to death. Just another dead kid. But here we've got snakes, a preacher."

That night, as I watched a television newscast about the trial on a station out of Chattanooga, I, too, was aware of the skewed priorities that drove the media. But to be honest, I also found myself more interested in the case of the snake-handling preacher than in the death of the child.

In their closing arguments the next day, both Lackey and Duke appeared to distance themselves from the Summerfords, perhaps because of the snake handling itself. "This is an extremely dysfunctional family," Mr. Lackey, Glenn's attorney, said. "It's hard for any of us to descend into an abyss filled with serpents and practices with which we are unfamiliar." Of Darlene, he said, "We don't know what to make of a person who takes photographs of snakes around in her purse."

Duke, the prosecutor, said, "We're not dealing with reasonable people." He implied that Darlene's seventh-grade education made it impossible for her to have dreamed up such a complicated scheme to get custody of her boy. The proof of her husband's guilt, his logic seemed to say, lay in the poverty of Darlene's imagination. What he left the jury with was something minor, a matter of syntax, really. It was contained in the suicide note that Darlene testified her husband had dictated and forced her to write.

Duke read the short note aloud and pointed out a curiously repetitive pattern: "Daddy was asleep. Daddy's asleep. Glenn is asleep."

"This is not a suicide note. This is an alibi note," he concluded. "This man was trying to build an alibi."

During the jury's deliberations, I caught up with Darlene Summerford in a dark hallway on the first floor of the courthouse. She was leaning against the wall and smoking a cigarette. Fair skinned and rangy, she was attractive in a raw-boned way. Her most striking features were her eyes, the pupils of which were wide open and nearly octagonal in shape.

"I'm fixing to get that girl yonder," she said, pointing her cigarette at Bobbie Sue Thompson, who was just then walking out the courthouse door. "She's one of Glenn's girlfriends. He promised to marry her the fourteenth of this month."

Darlene looked at me, and her eyes narrowed. "I didn't run around on him. I didn't have time." It had been Glenn who had done the running around, she said, and she went through a list of women she suspected he'd had affairs with. "If he'd straightened up, we could have had a good life," she added.

But it had never been much of a life for her, she said, even before she hooked up with Glenn Summerford. One of thirteen children born to a couple on disability in the Sand Mountain town of Dutton, she'd had to struggle for everything she'd had. One baby'd been taken away from her by the welfare people, and she had sworn then she'd never let another one go without a fight.

She started suspecting things weren't right between her and Glenn when he broke her mother's jaw with a vase at a family dinner and when he hit a brother-in-law over the head with a pair of vise grips shortly after that. And then there was the drinking and the fits of jealousy and his own infidelities, which he didn't admit to anybody. But she'd still prayed for him when he got bit by a western diamondback in the middle of July. She thought all along that he'd come to his senses and straighten himself out after that. Maybe then they'd have had a chance. But even if he'd seen the light, maybe even then it would have been too late. Darlene Summerford knew she was due for a change. She just didn't think it'd take the shape it did.

It had been only four months since she'd been bitten, but her life had already taken a turn for the better. She'd gotten a job at Andover Togs in Pisgah, a trailer next to her mother's house near Dutton, and a half acre of land. The doctor had told her the baby she was carrying was going to be all right. She said if she started going to church again, it'd be to a different kind, maybe Baptist. "I sure ain't gonna marry no preacher, though," she said.

In the meantime, she had her mind set on one thing. "I just want justice." And she stubbed her cigarette out on the sole of her shoe.

Several hours later, it came. The jury found Glenn guilty of attempted murder. The verdict was met in silence by a courtroom filled with people who did not seem to fully comprehend what was at stake. Because of prior convictions for grand larceny and burglary long before he took up preaching, Glenn faced the possibility of life in prison under

Alabama's Habitual Felony Offender Act. And that's exactly what happened. Judge Campbell later sentenced him to ninety-nine years in the state penitentiary.

The prosecutor had maintained during the proceedings that the trial was not about snake handling. But in ways that is all it had been about. Facing fear. Taking risks. Having faith.

"I knowed I was telling the truth," Darlene said after the trial. "I figured they'd say I was lying, but it didn't matter. I knowed I was telling the truth."

But what I would most remember from the trial was something Darlene Summerford said in the first floor hallway before the verdict came down. We were leaning against the wall while she smoked a cigarette, our heads close together so no one would overhear. I had asked her what it was like to take up serpents. She knew it was a serious question. She blew smoke thoughtfully toward the ceiling, and even after all she'd been through, there was a note of wistfulness in her voice when she finally said, "It makes you feel different. It's just knowing you got power over them snakes."

Power over them snakes. On the road back to Birmingham that night, I wondered exactly what she meant. I was in that fugue state familiar to most journalists, the exhausted aftermath of the legwork of an assignment, before the writing begins. The article about the trial, which I was composing in my head even then, had a predetermined shape and a natural end. Glenn Summerford had been convicted. Justice had prevailed. But the moment Darlene Summerford told me what it felt like to take up serpents, I knew the real story wouldn't be over until I'd seen and experienced what she was talking about for myself. Darlene's journey with the handlers was behind her now. Mine had just begun.

3
SHEEP
WITHOUT A
SHEPHERD

"I guess you heard about Brother Clyde," said Cecil Esslinder, the redheaded guitar player with the perpetual grin. We were standing on the square in Scottsboro a few weeks after Glenn Summerford's trial, and Cecil was squinting up at the noon-day sun.

"All I know is what I read in the papers," I said.

"That's what I'm talking about."

The papers had reported that on the Saturday night after Glenn's conviction, a man named Clyde Crossfield had been bitten by a rattlesnake at The Church of Jesus with Signs Following. He'd been flown by helicopter to a hospital in Chattanooga and had survived the bite, but some members of the church thought he wouldn't have been bitten in the first place if Glenn Summerford had been there to pray over the snake before he picked it up.

"Brother Clyde was acting crazy," Cecil said. "He just pulled that serpent out of the box and started jerkin' and swingin' it around like he was mad at it."

The rattlesnake bit Brother Clyde on one hand and hung on. When he managed to pry the snake off, it bit him on the other hand. Infuriated, he pulled the snake's fangs out of its mouth, put it back in the box, and sat down once more among the congregation. At first, it looked like he might be all right, Cecil said. But about twenty minutes later, he fell over onto the floor. That's when they sent for an ambulance.

"Brother Clyde wasn't anointed to take up that serpent," Cecil said. "You'd have to be crazy to go and pick up a snake like that."

"He didn't even pray over the box or nothing," said Cecil's wife, Carolyn, a short, pear-shaped woman who was leaning against their car while she tugged at a stubborn hangnail.

"Do you know Punkin Brown?" Cecil asked.

I shook my head.

"Brother Punkin is from Newport, Tennessee," he said. "Now there's a man who really gets anointed by the Holy Ghost. He'll get so carried away, he'll use a rattlesnake to wipe the sweat off his brow." Cecil paused and glanced around the square. "That Brother Clyde, though. He must have been a little mentally ill."

It happens all the time in the South — preachers leaving a church in disgrace. Most of the scandals are predictable and banal: illicit sex or the misuse of church funds. Few preachers leave their churches under circumstances as peculiar as Glenn Summerford's, and rarely have the dangers been so great for those left behind.

Cecil and Carolyn Esslinder had remained loyal to Glenn after his arrest and conviction. Other church members hadn't. Some had sided with Darlene. And still others, who had stood by Glenn after his arrest, became disillusioned with his behavior and left the church even before the trial began. Among them were Sylvia and Johnny Ingram, who had been attending the church for about three years. Johnny, a sheet metal contractor who had made a rare leap to the middle class, had been the church treasurer and had paid for Glenn's lawyer. "We loved the preacher," said his wife, Sylvia. But when Johnny's sister-in-law, Tammy Flippo, left her husband and children to visit Glenn while he was free on bond after his arrest, Johnny and Sylvia had a change of heart. "We didn't choose to go to a church where the preacher did one thing and preached another," Sylvia said.

The tensions between those who sided with Glenn and those who sided with Darlene exploded in bitter name-calling on the day of the hearing to determine who would get custody of the Summerfords' teenage son, Marty. Although the hearing was closed to the public, the hall outside was packed with supporters of both Glenn and Darlene. No blows were exchanged, but occasionally someone from one side or the other would have to pass through a gauntlet of catcalls and icy stares. It was uncomfortable even for an outsider like me to cross the line and talk to both sides.

"They're nothing but a bunch of liars, thieves, adulterers, and hypocrites," Darlene said to me as she glowered at the church members who had remained loyal to Glenn. She accused them of having taken many of her personal belongings from the house on Barbee Lane, including her pet bird, a cockatiel. "They even stole my underwear," she said.

A reluctant witness on Glenn's behalf paced the opposite end of the corridor. He was waiting to be called into the hearing room. He said he had known Darlene's family, the Collinses, for over twenty years. "It was a house full of sluts then, and that's what they are today," he whispered.

In an alcove off the hall, under the watchful eye of an armed sheriff's deputy, Glenn Summerford himself sat brooding in his white prison garb. His eyes looked hooded and remote. "I didn't even know she *had* a bird," he told me. It was Darlene and her supporters, he insisted, who had taken everything. "They brought a truck and stole a bunch of church equipment, several hundred dollars worth."

Predictably, Glenn's version of the events that had landed him in prison also differed from Darlene's. He said that he didn't even know she'd gotten bit by a snake on the night of October 5. "I loved her," he said. "I didn't try to kill her. I kept her from killing herself."

In the weeks prior to that night, they had both backslid and taken to drink, he said. "She was bad to run around," he added. "On September eighteenth I caught her with a man, a preacher from the church. When I told her on October fifth I wanted to get a divorce, she tried to kill herself."

He said she took a box of Sominex and a bottle of extra-strength Tylenol. He made her drink warm water so she'd throw the pills up. She threatened to kill him. It was a similar story to the one the jury had heard in snatches during the trial, but not from Glenn's own mouth. On the advice of counsel, he hadn't testified in his own defense. "If there's a new trial, I'll testify," he said.

About that time, he craned his neck to peer down the hallway, where those supporting him and those supporting Darlene had coalesced into the two opposing camps. He couldn't have seen Darlene from there, but he shook his head sadly as though he had. "She'd completely backslid," he said.

Then he leaned closer to me. "I looked at her at the trial. She looked spiritually dead. When Darlene was living right, she looked clean, nice. Afterwards, she just looked dead."

We talked for a while longer, and then I asked him if he'd ever drunk strychnine in church. "I've drank it different times," he said.

"What about Darlene?"

"When she was really living right, she drank it," he said.

When she was really living right, she drank poison. What a peculiar idea, the journalist in me thought. But who was I to judge?

I never intended to become a journalist. I wanted to be a forest ranger. In college, though, I took fiction writing courses instead of forestry, and after a stint in the army, I went to graduate school at the University of Iowa Writers' Workshop. I had it in my head that I would write short stories and teach at a good liberal arts college somewhere in the Midwest.

After some detours, that's exactly what happened. I wound up at The College of Wooster in Ohio. I was on my second marriage by then, to the sister of a childhood friend. Vicki, too, was from Birmingham and a writer, although she didn't fully know it yet. She was employed in Ohio as a social worker and had just written her first short story. She hated the Ohio winters. I hated academic life. I decided I wanted to turn thirty unemployed in an apartment back in Birmingham. Writing would be my living from now on. The idea had a romantic ring. It was a wonderful moment when we quit our jobs, thumbed our noses at common sense, and headed south again. We felt like we'd committed the ultimate rebellion: We'd taken our lives into our own hands.

Things worked out all right at first. I did turn thirty unemployed in an apartment in a Birmingham neighborhood called Southside. Vicki found work as a therapist in a substance abuse program at the university there. I sure wasn't making a living as a writer, though, so I began teaching part-time at the university. We decided to have children. Vicki conceived quickly, but lost the baby and nearly died herself. We thought we'd never be able to have children after that. And like many childless couples our age, we sank into cynicism and carelessness. Or should I say, we drank ourselves there, something we'd been doing for a number of years. But both of us continued to write. Our stories occasionally appeared in the literary magazines, and I wrote a novel that was rejected at a couple of houses before it wound up in a box under my bed.

A kind of desperation set in. I felt like my writing wasn't going anywhere, and my job as a college English teacher seemed minor and absurd. I wanted to have an adventure before I turned thirty-five, one in which the risks were real. I'd been in the army during Vietnam, but I hadn't been sent overseas. Maybe I felt like I hadn't proven myself as a man. My education as a writer wasn't complete. In 1983, I decided I wanted to go to a war, and the nearest one was in El Salvador. Journalism seemed the logical means. I borrowed a thousand dollars from my credit union, found a photographer, David Donaldson, who also wanted to go, and talked the editor of a Birmingham newspaper into giving us press credentials. I'd never written a word for a newspaper. I'd never been out of the United States. The only Spanish I knew was "I am a journalist. Please don't shoot me."

I became a journalist in El Salvador. And something else happened to me down there. It was more than learning a new trade and a new language. In El Salvador, I found the antidote for a conventional life: I got the shit scared out of me. I haven't been the same since. On the plane down, I read an article about John Sullivan, a free-lance journalist who, on his first night in El Salvador, had been taken from his hotel by armed men, tortured, beheaded, and buried in a wall. At the airport, armed customs police confiscated my binoculars and Boy Scout canteen. Our taxi driver barely got us into the city before the curfew began. Outside our hotel, security forces with automatic weapons were stopping and searching cars at random. The phones at the hotel were tapped.

On my first trip into the countryside, I went with other journalists to a town that had been overrun by guerrillas.

Walking down the cobbled streets, I could hear the clatter of machine-gun fire and the steady *whump* of mortar rounds. The guerrillas we encountered demanded "war taxes," which we paid. That night, in the hotel lounge, a man came up to our table, accused us of being American military officers, and asked us to accompany him outside. He said he had a gun in his back pocket, and if we didn't come with him, he would kill us on the spot. Hotel security got to him and hustled him away. There was no gun in his back pocket, but he'd achieved the desired effect.

After that first trip, I quit drinking. So did Vicki. The second time I went to El Salvador, she went with me. While she stayed at the hotel, I rode into the countryside and interviewed the fighters on both sides in the civil war. Both suspected I was a spy. At night Vicki and I would lie awake listening to the sound of gunfire and exploding grenades. During dinner one night at the home of friends, we had to crawl under the table when shooting erupted on the street outside.

When I returned to El Salvador for the fourth time, Vicki was pregnant with our first daughter, Ashley. On that visit, in September of 1984, photographer Jim Neel and I were interviewing guerrillas along the road to a town called La Palma, in the northern province of Chalatenango. While we were talking to a guerrilla commander, a Salvadoran army patrol opened fire. The guerrillas scattered like quail. Jim and I dove for a drainage ditch. The gunfire was unrelenting and close. The air above our heads was filled with bullets. And time very nearly stopped. Jim watched an insect move slowly along my shoulder, and I found myself staring at the water pouring out of a culvert and into the ditch. The water was frothy with raw sewage, but the light falling upon it mesmerized me. Like the other physical sensations — the sucking sound my boots made in the mud, the hum of insects, the sting of sweat — the light on the water was precious to me, as though it were something I knew I was about to lose.

We were in that ditch for half an hour. I was certain we were going to die. For the first time, I realized how much I wanted to live. I was shameless in this prayer of mine. I promised everything. We made it out alive, but altered. During the next six years, I went back to Central America again and again, a dozen times in all. I was always scared. Ashley and our second daughter, Laura, were born during those years. Vicki's writing career took off. I survived turning forty, the death of my father, and a battle for tenure at the university. Nine years after I wrote it, that novel under my bed found a publisher. And shortly afterward, my father came back to me in a dream. My mother and sister had gone to the cemetery to lay flowers at his grave. When they returned, he was with them. He had a message for our family. "Jesus found our lives here too beautiful," he said, "and so invented trials from which only he could save us by his act of continual self-sacrifice. Be that as it may," he concluded, "the love of God surpasses all others."

There was mystery and passion in the message, words my father might not have used in real life, though he often prayed aloud with uncommon eloquence. I did not take the dream lightly. I took it as a blessing. One thing was certain: My father had come back to me for a reason.

On Sundays, I would sit with Vicki on the back pew of an urban Southern Baptist church in Birmingham, the one she'd grown up in. It had Doric columns and an enormous Wedgwood blue sanctuary lighted by Italian chandeliers. The windows had been handcrafted in England. The organ made use of over three thousand pipes. I was grateful to be back in church, but I was also vaguely uncomfortable. The previous nine years had been a journey out of cynicism and denial into a kind of light. I had my life, my family, my sobriety. But something was missing. I had reached that point in the middle of looking for something when you have forgotten what it is you have lost. At the time, I couldn't have put it into words, but I think what I was looking for was what I had experienced growing up in that odd Methodist church in East Lake. I wanted some hoarse and perspiring preacher from the sticks to reach into his pocket and take out a comb.

And that was my spiritual condition on that day in 1992

when I left Glenn Summerford sitting in his white prison jumpsuit and made my way down the crowded corridor toward the light at the other end. Glenn's mother, Aunt Annie Mance, was standing in the crowd, and she recognized me from services at The Church of Jesus with Signs Following. She knew I was a journalist, but she smiled anyway. "We've missed you in church," she said as I passed, and then she added to some of her friends behind her: "We're going to make a snake handler out of him yet."

In a surprise development, Glenn Summerford won the custody battle. Since the day of the first murder attempt on Darlene, Marty had been staying with one of Glenn's daughters by a previous marriage. He had been doing well in school. Apparently, the judge decided it would be in Marty's best interests to stay where he was until his father got out of prison, a long wait, considering Glenn had been sentenced to ninety-nine years. The ruling was a blow to Darlene and her family, but only a bittersweet victory for Glenn's supporters within The Church of Jesus with Signs Following. They had their own problems to worry about by now, problems that would eventually result in a dramatic split over finances and church authority.

In the weeks before the attack on Darlene, Glenn had quit the church. In a tearful confession, he said he'd backed up on the Lord and wasn't fit to pastor the church anymore. J.L. Dyal, the man with the Jesus belt buckle, tried to keep the church going by making sure the utilities got paid and the doors were open for scheduled services. Visiting preachers, including Carl Porter, took up the slack in Glenn's absence. But after Darlene was bitten by the snakes, Glenn called Carl Porter in Georgia and asked him to come to Scottsboro to rebaptize him. Brother Carl, who had first heard about the attack on a television newscast, agreed to perform the baptism. "He said he'd come back to the Lord," Brother Carl recalled.

Glenn also asked Brother Carl to call Darlene at the university hospital in Birmingham and try to persuade her to patch things up. Glenn's own trip to the hospital on the day after the attack had ended disastrously when he was met in Birmingham by university police, who arrested him on a DUI charge and confiscated a handgun.

Brother Carl made the call to Darlene's hospital room, but she refused Glenn's peace offer, choosing to press charges of attempted murder instead. Glenn was despondent. Having been rebaptized, he preached again at the church until the trial, but after his conviction, the responsibility of keeping the church going fell again to J.L. Dyal. "Glenn asked me to keep the doors open on the church and I was doing everything I could to do it," J.L. says. "It was kind of rough, but I did the best I could. I'd go down there and we'd pray and I'd read a verse or two out of the Bible. I didn't call myself a preacher."

Brother Carl came to Scottsboro as often as he could, but he was too busy with his own church in Georgia to pastor the Scottsboro church, too. He did take up a collection, though, to help with Glenn's legal expenses, and then turned the money over to J.L. The final crisis began brewing when J.L. went to visit Glenn in jail, and Glenn told him to turn that money over to Tammy Flippo, the surprise defense witness whom in-laws described as a woman who had left her husband and children in order to be with Glenn.

"I said no," says J.L. "That money's for your lawyer."

"Tammy's gonna get me another lawyer," Glenn said.

"No she ain't, Brother Glenn," J.L. said. "She's gonna rip you off." But against his better judgment, J.L. says he gave in.

"From now on," Glenn told him later, "whenever you pick up a donation or anything at the church, I want you to give it to Tammy."

This time, J.L. was adamant. "I can't do that," he said.

"Well, if you're not going to help me when I need help," Glenn said, "you might as well close the doors on the church."

J.L. said, "Maybe I had better do that."

The two men talked it over. Glenn finally said he wanted J.L. to keep the church going, and J.L. said he would. "Me and my wife were handling the collection," J.L. says. "We were paying the bills. We kept records of everything we did. I mean, we accounted for every penny of it."

But that was not the end of the pressure to divert the offering at The Church of Jesus with Signs Following. That spring a letter addressed to the congregation arrived, supposedly written from jail by Glenn. "He wanted his mother and Bobbie Sue Thompson to take over the treasury," Brother Carl Porter said.

That's how J.L. remembers it, too. "I said I ain't gonna do it. And they said, well, here's the letter right here, you know, and I said I'm sorry. At the time there wasn't nobody paying tithes down there but me and Brother Willie and Mama and my wife, Dorothea, and Brother Porter. They said, well, we'll have the law to get it from you. I said you send the law out here and if they can get it, I'll give it to 'em."

J.L. is leaning forward in the living room of his house on Sand Mountain. His fingers are knit, and he's looking at a framed print on the wall of Jesus appearing in the sky above a waterfall. "The night I walked out down there, I told them, I said, 'Well, I'm no longer a member here.' And come to find out, Brother Glenn didn't write the letter to start with." J.L. now believed that the letter had been written by Bobbie Sue.

When J.L. left the church, Brother Carl decided that he'd stop trying to keep it open, too.

For all practical purposes, it was the end of The Church of Jesus with Signs Following. The miniature steeple with the wooden cross would come down and lie in the grass behind the house on Barbee Lane, near the shed where Glenn Summerford had kept the rattlesnakes that he had tried to murder Darlene with. Some of the pews would be stacked up and left to rot in a nearby hollow under the trees. On a Sunday after this final split, Vicki and I drove up from Birmingham. I had wanted her to experience firsthand what went on there during worship services, but we found the walls of the church bare, no portraits of Jesus, no Last Supper. There were no amplifiers, no set of drums, no microphone, cymbals, or tambourines. There were no bottles of oil, no jars of strychnine, no propane torches, no snakes. Glenn's mother, Aunt Annie, was there with Cecil and Carolyn Esslinder, loyal to the end. Also present was a Brother Tony with his family. New to the area, they'd just been driving around looking for a place where they could worship when they spotted the converted service station with its hand-painted sign.

"Brother Carl's not coming back no more," Aunt Annie said. "He wanted us to give our tithes to J.L., but I didn't want to give mine to anybody but a preacher, and J.L.'s no preacher." Her eyes were still giving her trouble from recent cataract surgery, and when she took off her tinted glasses to clean them, she had to squint against the light. "Glenn needs some spending money at the jail, and I'd like to see some tithes go to him, but Brother Carl said no, if we didn't give the tithes to J.L., he wouldn't be back, and he hasn't been."

Brother Tony had brought along his brother, a stooped, walleyed man who struck up a chorus of "Jesus on My Mind" on his battered acoustic guitar. His strumming hand appeared palsied, but the music came out strong and sure.

"I told Glenn about all this," Aunt Annie said in a louder voice. "He said, 'Don't worry, Mama, they'll be a preacher there this evening.' And sure enough, when I got here, here was Brother Tony."

The meeting started to sound like an actual service. Having come to the front of the church, Brother Tony sang with gusto. He'd seen now that he'd been led by the Lord to this place and this time. "I believe in snake handling!" he shouted when the song had ended. "I've been bit myself! I don't shake the box down or look for the heads! I just reach in and take one out!" He made a dramatic, downward sweeping gesture with his hand, as though there were a real box in front of him, with a real live rattlesnake buzzing angrily inside.

"If you have to shake the box or look to see where its head is at," he continued, "you ought'n be trying to get that snake out of that box in the first place!"

Cecil and Aunt Annie gave him a few amens, but it was clear their hearts weren't totally into it. They knew they had come to the end of one thing and the beginning of something else. Without real serpents present, what was the point of talking about them?

In time, regular worship services would recommence in the converted service station on Woods Cove Road. It'd be known by a different name though: Woods Cove Holiness Church. And no snakes would be handled there. Aunt Annie's health would deteriorate to the point where she would rarely get to church, anyway. And her boy, Glenn, would continue to spend his days and nights spreading the gospel to fellow prisoners at a state penitentiary west of Birmingham.

Offerings at the church had routinely been twelve to fifteen dollars a service, and it was over amounts like these that the remnant of church members who believed in Glenn's innocence split. The issue was one of church authority, which in the free Holiness tradition resides entirely with the pastor. A further principle had been at stake, though. Would the church be run from prison or not? J.L. and his family had spoken with their feet.

The eventual outcome was that snake handling ceased at The Church of Jesus with Signs Following in Scottsboro, but started up, as soon as the weather permitted, in an open field

on top of Sand Mountain, where Brother Carl Porter, J.L.
Dyal, and the End-Time Evangelist, Brother Charles
McGlocklin, would lead services under muscadine vines, hon-
eysuckle, and starlight, like believers used to do in the old
days, before the world with all its deceitfulness and vanities
lured them down from the mountains and into the city, where
a woman might be tempted to back up on the Lord and stop
drinking strychnine, and her husband would have to take
matters into his own hands by putting a gun to her head and
forcing her to reach into the serpent box.

4
UNDER THE BRUSH ARBOR

———

The card he pressed into my hand read: "Charles McGlocklin, the End-Time Evangelist. " "You can have as much of God as you want," he said. His voice was low and urgent. "These seminary preachers don't understand that. They don't understand the spirit of the Lord. They're taught by man. They know the *forms* of godliness, but they deny the *power*."

Brother Charles was a big man in his early fifties with a full head of dark hair and hands the size of waffle irons. He didn't have a church himself, and he didn't particularly want one. He'd preached on the radio, he said, and at county fairs and trade days. In years past, he'd driven all over the South, conducting revivals under a tent he'd hauled in the back of his '72 Chevy van. He said he had even stood on the road in front of his house trailer in New Hope, Alabama, and preached at passing cars.

"I get a lot of stares," he added, and then he put his big hand on my shoulder and drew me toward him confidentially. "I have received visitations by angels," he said. "One of them was seven feet tall. It was a frightening experience."

I said I bet it was.

"And I'll tell you something else," he said. "One night I was fasting and praying on the mountain, and I was taken out in the spirit. The Lord appeared to me in layers of light." His grip tightened on my shoulder. "He spoke a twelve-hour message to me on one word: *polluted.*"

"Polluted?"

"Yes. Polluted. Now, you think about that for a minute. A twelve-hour message."

I thought about it for a minute, and then decided Brother Charles was out of his mind.

In time, I'd find out he wasn't, despite the fact that he kept four copperheads in a terrarium on his kitchen counter between the Mr. Coffee and the microwave. He said God moved on him one night to handle a big timber rattler right there in the kitchen. His wife, Aline, showed me a photo of him doing it. Aline was thirteen years younger than Charles, childlike and frankly beautiful, a Holiness mystic from Race

Track Road who worked the night shift weaving bandage gauze. "I had just got up, getting ready to go to work," she said, "and my camera was just laying there." She pointed at the photo. "You see how the Holy Ghost moved on him?"

In the photo, Charles is standing in the kitchen in his white T-shirt and jeans. He has a rattlesnake in one hand, and he appears to be shouting at it as though it were a sensible and rebellious thing. "There's serpents, and then there's *fiery* serpents," Charles said. "That one was a fiery serpent."

Another time, Charles said he wanted to take up a serpent real bad, but he didn't have one on hand. The Holy Ghost told him, "You don't have a snake, but you've got a heater." So Charles ran to the wood-burning stove in the living room and laid his hands on it. "Baby, that thing was hot," he said. But his hands, when he finally took them off the stove, weren't a bit burned. Instead, they were as cold as a block of ice, he said.

Aline reminded him that he *did* get a blister from a skillet once, but Charles said, "God wasn't in that. That was in myself. That's why I got burned."

"You were just thinking about that corn bread," Aline added with a knowing smile.

Long before I was a guest in their home, I'd seen the McGlocklins at services at The Church of Jesus with Signs Following in Scottsboro. We became friends, and then something more than friends, but that is a long and complicated

story that began, I think, on the afternoon of my first brush-
arbor meeting on top of Sand Mountain, when Aline was
taken out in the spirit, and I accompanied her on tambourine.

I had never even heard of a brush arbor until J.L. Dyal built
one in a field behind his house near the Sand Mountain town
of Section in the summer of 1992. Brother Carl had invited
me to the services, and J.L. had drawn a map. "You take a left
at the Sand Mountain Dragway sign," he said. "We'll get
started just before sundown."

I was pleased the handlers had felt comfortable enough to
include me. It meant the work was going well. The relationship between journalist and subject is often an unspoken con-
spiracy. The handlers wanted to show me something, and I
was ready to be shown. It seemed to me that the conviction of
Glenn Summerford was not the end of their story, but simply
the beginning of another chapter. I was interested in what
would happen to them now that Glenn was in prison and The
Church of Jesus with Signs Following had split. But I had a
personal agenda too. I was enjoying the passion and abandon of their worship. Vicki didn't seem to mind. She encouraged me to go. So I told Brother Carl and J.L. I'd be there for
the brush-arbor services, although I couldn't visualize what
they were talking about. "Brush arbor" seemed a contradic-
tory term. The word *arbor* suggested civilized restraint. The
word *brush* didn't.

I did know that outdoor revivals had once been common-
place in the rural South. The most famous occurred in 1801,
when thousands of renegade Presbyterians, in their rebellion
against stiff-necked Calvinism, gathered in a field near Cane
Ridge, Kentucky, for a week-long camp meeting. They were
soon joined by Methodists and Baptists, until their combined
ranks swelled to more than twenty-five thousand, a crowd
many times greater than the population of the largest town
in Kentucky at the time. Something inexplicable and porten-
tous happened to many of the worshipers in that field near
Cane Ridge. Overcome by the Holy Spirit, they began to
shriek, bark, and jerk. Some fell to the ground as though
struck dead. "Though so awful to behold," wrote one witness, "I do not remember that any one of the thousands . . .
ever sustained an injury in body."

Cane Ridge set the stage for the dramatic events at a mission on Azusa Street in Los Angeles in 1906, when the Holy
Ghost descended in power on a multiracial congregation led
by a one-eyed black preacher named William Seymour, and
the great American spiritual phenomenon of the twentieth
century, Pentecostalism, began in a fury of tongue speaking
and prophesying and healing.

Cane Ridge had been the prototype of revivalism on a
grand scale. The crowd at J.L.'s brush arbor was somewhat
smaller — thirteen of us altogether, plus a gaggle of curious

onlookers who hid behind Brother Carl Porter's Dodge Dakota pickup. But the facilities at J.L.'s were top-notch. Traditional brush arbors had been small and temporary, primitive shelters usually built at harvest time from whatever materials might be at hand. Willow branches were especially prized because of their flexibility. Thick vines added strength. The idea was to give field hands a place to worship so they wouldn't have to leave the premises before all the crops were in. But J.L. had constructed his brush arbor out of sturdy two-by-fours over which he had stretched sheets of clear plastic so that services could be held even in a downpour. The vines and brush piled on top of the plastic appeared to be decorative rather than functional, yielding the impression of a brush arbor without all its inconveniences. J.L.'s father-in-law, Dozier Edmonds, had helped string electricity to the structure and had installed a length of track lighting. The place was perfect, except for one thing. There weren't any snakes.

"I thought you were going to bring them," said Brother Carl to Brother Charles.

"I thought Brother Willie was going to bring them," Charles replied. He was getting his guitar out of the car, an instrument the Lord, he said, had taught him to play.

"Brother Willie got serpent bit last night," Carl reminded him.

"I know, but he said he was going to be here today."

"Maybe I need to check on him after the service," Carl said. "It was a copperhead," he confided to me. "Over in Georgia. Bit him on the thumb, but it didn't hurt him bad."

"Well, we don't *have* to have serpents to worship the Lord," Charles finally said. He put his boot up on a pine bench that would serve as the altar and began strumming the guitar. When everyone had gathered around, he started to sing. *"He's God in Alabama. He's God in Tennessee. He's God in North Carolina. He's God all over me. Oh, God is God . . . and Jesus is his name. . . ."*

The service had begun at five o'clock to avoid the mid-afternoon heat. The light was low and golden over the field, and Charles's voice rose above it like a vapor, unamplified, snatched away by the breeze. Aline was there; Brother Carl and the old prophetess, Aunt Daisy; J.L. and his wife, Dorothea; one of their daughters-in-law and her baby; and Dorothea's father, Dozier, and her mother, Burma, who had a twin sister named Erma. Both Burma and Erma, sixty-eight, attended snake-handling services, usually in identical dresses, but only Burma actually handled.

I'd also brought photographers Jim Neel and Melissa Springer with me, and they moved quietly around the edges of the arbor as the service picked up steam. The choice of photographers had been simple. Jim was one of my oldest friends. In addition to being a sculptor and painter, he'd worked with me as a combat photographer in Central America during the

1980s. Melissa, whose work I'd first noticed when it was censored by police at an outdoor exhibit in Birmingham, had been documenting the lives of men and women clinging to the underbelly of the American dream — female impersonators, dancers with AIDS, women inmates in the HIV isolation unit at Alabama's Julia Tutwiler prison. When I told her about the snake handlers, she said she had to meet them, but unlike most people who say they want to, she kept calling and insisting that we set a time. She and Jim were an interesting study in contrasts: He was moody, private, and intense; Melissa was warm, expansive, and maternal. But both were obsessed with their work, easy to travel with, and open to possibilities.

Melissa had worn an ankle-length dress this time. At her first service in Scottsboro, she'd gotten the message when Aunt Daisy prophesied against the wearing of pants by women. Outsiders are bound to get preached at a little in Holiness churches. But the same Holiness preachers who draw attention to unorthodox details of behavior or dress inevitably hugged us after the service and invited us back.

Some preachers didn't take the Holiness prescriptions about dress quite as seriously as others. Charles McGlocklin's theory was simple: "You've got to catch the fish before you clean them."

His wife, Aline, didn't wear makeup or cut her hair, but she occasionally allowed herself the luxury of a brightly colored hair ornament. "God looks at the heart, anyway. He doesn't look on the outside," she said. She also drove a white Chevy Beretta with an airbrushed tag that read "Aline loves Charles." Charles's pickup had a matching tag, with "Charles loves Aline." Both sentiments were inscribed in the middle of interlocking hearts, like the brightly colored hearts on Aline's hair clasp.

Despite the empty chairs and the lack of electric guitars or serpents, the worship at J.L.'s brush arbor followed the same pattern I'd experienced in Scottsboro. Without church walls, it seemed more delicate and temporal, though, and Brother Carl's sermon echoed the theme. He talked about the flesh as grass, passing in a moment, of earthly life being short and illusory. He talked about the body as "fleshy rags" that he would gladly give up in exchange for a heavenly wardrobe. But at the center of Carl's sermon was the topic of God's love, which he seemed to first discover fully even as he talked his way into it.

"It's got no end," he said, "no bottom, no ceiling. Paul says nothing can separate us from the love of God through Jesus Christ. And let me tell you, sometimes we find His love in the little things. The fact that we're here today is a sign God loves us." *Amen.* "The fact that we got a brain to think with, and a tongue to speak with, and a song to sing. I just want to thank Him for waking me up this morning," he said. "I want to thank Him for giving me food to eat and a roof over my head. Sometimes we ask Him to work big miracles, but forget to thank Him for the little ones." *Amen*. "But he's a great big God, and He never fails. His grace is sufficient to meet our every need. He's a good God, isn't He?" And everybody said amen.

Then Carl invited Brother Charles to give his testimony. In Holiness churches, a testimony is a personal story that reveals God's power and grace. It's not meant to exhort or instruct the congregation — that would be preaching — but simply to praise the Lord. In practice, though, the line between testifying and preaching is not so clear-cut.

Brother Carl and Brother Charles hugged, and after a few introductory comments about the beauty of the afternoon and the love he felt from everybody gathered there, Brother Charles began to testify. It was a story, both lurid and familiar, that could only have come from the South.

"Up until I was five years old," Charles said, "I lived in a tent on the banks of the Tennessee River at Old Whitesburg Bridge. Y'all know where that's at. Then my mother got remarried, and we moved to a houseboat at Clouds Cove."

Clouds Cove.

"My stepdaddy was a drunk."

"Amen," said J.L., who knew something about drunks himself.

"My real daddy lived to be eighty," Charles said. "He died in the Tennessee penitentiary, where he was serving a life sentence for killing his second wife. I was like a lamb

thrown into a den of lions when we moved to Clouds Cove,"
Charles said. "In 1948, when I was six, we lived on nothing
but parched corn for three weeks, like rats. We slept on grass
beds. We didn't even have a pinch of salt. Now, that's poor."

Amen. They all knew what it was like to be poor.

"By the time I was eight, I'd seen two men killed in our
house. I was afraid to go to sleep at night."

Help him, Jesus.

"I made it to the eighth grade, but when I was just shy of
turning thirteen years old, I got shot in the stomach with a
twelve-gauge shotgun. That was the first time I heard the
audible voice of God."

Praise His holy name!

"There I was, holding my insides in my hands. Them
things, they really colored up funny, I thought to myself. Then
I had the awfullest fear come up on me," Charles said. He was
pacing back and forth by now, a loping, methodical pace, his
huge, dog-eared Bible held loosely in one hand like an imple-
ment. "I saw a vision of my casket lid closing on me, and the
voice out of heaven spoke to me and said, 'Don't be afraid,
'cause everything's gonna be all right,' and I felt that shield
of faith just come down on me!"

Hallelujah!

"God's been good to me!"

Amen.

"He's been good to me!"

Amen.

"Doctors told my mother I had maybe fifteen minutes to live. 'There's no way he can make it,' they said. 'Almost all his liver's shot out, almost all his stomach.' I was on the operating table sixteen to eighteen hours. They had to take out several *yards* of intestines. I stayed real bad for forty-two days and nights. I was one hundred twenty pounds when I got shot and eighty-seven when I got out of that hospital. But just look at me now!"

Praise His name!

Brother Charles was standing with his hands clenched at his side and a wild look in his eyes. He was a big man, an enormous man. It was not the first time I'd noticed that, but it was the first time I had considered the damage he might do if he ever had a reason.

"God's been good to me!" he said as he started pacing again.

Amen.

"I said He's been good to me!"

Amen!

He suddenly stopped in his tracks. "But I wasn't always good to Him."

"Now you're telling it," Brother Carl said.

"When I was sixteen, I went to live with my real daddy in Tennessee," Charles said. "He was one of the biggest moonshiners in the state, and I wanted to learn the trade. I dabbled in it a good long time. I was bad. I went up to Chicago and did some other things I shouldn't have."

Tell it. They'd all done things they shouldn't have.

"When I came back South, I drove a long-haul rig twice a week to New York City. Then I bought me a thirty-three acre farm in Minor Hill, Tennessee. Two-story house. Fine car. I had a still upstairs that could run forty to fifty gallons of whiskey, and in another room I stored my bales of marijuana. Pretty good for a boy who'd grown up picking cotton."

Amen. They knew about cotton.

He raised his Bible and shook it at us. "I don't have to tell you that's the deceitfulness of riches talking, boys."

Preach on.

"One day, things had really got bad on me. I had just got under so much that I couldn't go no further, and I was getting ready to kill myself. The devil spoke to me and said, 'Just go ahead and take that gun and kill yourself and get it over with'"

No, Lord.

He walked to the edge of the arbor and pantomimed picking something up from the grass. "I went over there and got the gun and was fixing to put a shell in it, and when I did, this other voice came to me and said, 'Put that gun back down and walk back over in front of that wood heater.'"

Amen.

"I walked back over there in front of the wood heater, and suddenly that power from on high hit me in the head and knocked me down on my knees, and I said six words. I won't never forget what they was. I said, 'Lord, have mercy on my soul.'"

Amen. Thank God.

"He took me out in the Spirit and I came back speaking in other tongues as the Spirit gave utterance. The devil said, 'Look, look now. Now what are you going to do?' He said, 'Look at all that moonshine, all that marijuana you got. What are you going to do now? Ain't you in a mess now? Here you are, you've got the Holy Ghost, and you've got all *this* in your house.' And the Lord spoke to me and said, 'Just set your house in order.'"

Bless him, Lord!

"He said, 'Just set your house in order!'"

Amen!

"So that's what I did. I set my house in order. I got rid of that moonshine and marijuana. I told the devil to depart that place in the name of Jesus, and within a year I'd taken up my first serpent."

Amen.

"We've got to set our house in order!" Charles said, and now he was leaning toward us, red-faced, with flecks of white spittle in the corners of his mouth. "We're in the last day with the Lord, children! He won't strive with man forever! He's a merciful God, he's a loving God, but you better believe he's also a just God, and there will come a time when we'll have to account for these lives we've led! We better put our house in order!"

Amen. Thank God. Bless the sweet name of Jesus.

There were only thirteen people under that brush arbor, but it seemed like there were suddenly three hundred. They were jumping and shouting, and pretty soon Brother Carl was anointing Burma and Erma with oil, and Brother Charles had launched into "Jesus on My Mind" on his guitar, and J.L. and I had our tambourines going. There was so much racket that at first it was hard to hear what Aline was doing over in the corner by a length of dog wire that the morning glory vines had twined around. Her back was to us. Her hands were in the air, and she was rocking slowly from side to side, her face upturned and her voice quavering, "Akiii, akiii, akiii. Akiii, akiii, akiii. . . ."

It was the strangest sound I had ever heard. At first, it did not seem human. It sounded like the voice of a rare night bird, or some tiny feral mammal. And then the voice got louder, mounting up on itself, until it started to sound like that of a child who was lost and in great pain. But even as the hairs on my arm started to stand on end, the voice turned into something else, a sound that had pleasure in it as well as torment. Ecstasy, I would learn later, is excruciating, but I did not know that then.

"Akiii, akiii, akiii. . . ." The singing and praising elsewhere in the brush arbor had started to diminish. Brother Charles had stopped strumming his guitar. Brother Carl had put away his oil. Burma and Dorothea kept their hands raised, but except for an occasional amen or praise Jesus, the air fell silent around Aline's voice. Everyone was listening to her now. I could not disentangle myself from the sound of her voice, the same syllables repeated with endless variation. At times, it seemed something barbed was being pulled from her throat; at other times, the sound was a clear stream flowing outward into thin air. Her voice seemed to be right in my ear. It was a sobbing. A panting after something she could not quite reach. And then it would be a coming to rest in some exquisite space, a place so tender it could not be touched without "Akiii, akiii, akiii. . . ." The sun had set and the electric lights were not yet turned on, but the arbor seemed filled with a golden light. We were swaying in it, transfixed, with Aline silhouetted against the dog wire and the morning glory vines. All but her trembling voice was silent, or so it seemed, until I realized with horror that my tambourine was still going, vibrating against my leg, almost apart from me, as if it had a motive and direction of its own.

My hand froze. It was as though I had been caught in

some act of indecency. But Aline's voice reacted with renewed desperation, "Akiii, akiii, akiii," and so I let the tambourine have its own way, now louder and faster, until it almost burst into a song, and then softer and more slowly, until it resembled the buzzing of a rattlesnake in a serpent box. It anticipated every move that Aline's voice made, and vice versa. The intimacy was unnerving: her voice and the tambourine, perfectly attuned to one another and moving toward the same end. I was unreasonably afraid that Charles would be angry with me. I didn't yet know the full dimensions of passion. It was much later that I would come to understand what had gone on in that moment. The tambourine was simply accompanying Aline while she felt for and found God. And I mean "accompany" in its truest sense: "to occur with." And nobody could predict when something like that might happen. Through the tambourine, I was occurring with her in the Spirit, and it was not of my own will.

I cannot say how long the episode lasted. It seemed to go on for a very long time. J.L. turned the lights on at the end. The men hugged the men. The women hugged the women. Aline and I shook hands. If the snake handlers found anything unusual about our curious duet afterward, they never spoke directly to me about it. But I do know one thing: It was after that brush-arbor meeting on Sand Mountain that they started to call me Brother Dennis.

5
JOLO

By late summer I was feeling comfortable among the handlers. In fact, I was getting restless in my home church in Birmingham, where I'd occasionally want to put my hands up in the air. I didn't. But sometimes I'd tap my feet during the choir's anthem or mumble an amen or two. And I was pretty much obsessed with snake handling, though I had not, in fact, handled one myself. When Jim and Melissa and I found ourselves at a party together, we'd get off in the corner and talk about the handlers, especially Aline McGlocklin, whose childlike beauty continued to arrest and mystify us. She always seemed to be on the verge of ecstasy. Sometimes, she said, the Lord would move on her in the ladies room at work. We'd never seen her take up a serpent, though, and we wondered if we ever would. Other friends in Birmingham started to ask about the services. Some of them wanted to go. But soon the brush-arbor meetings would be over. The nights would turn cool. It rains on Sand Mountain in the fall, and there's fog. Without a church building of their own, the handlers would have to travel more often to Brother Carl's church in Georgia, or to churches in East Tennessee, Kentucky, or West Virginia.

"You going up to Jolo?" Brother Carl asked me after one of the brush-arbor meetings behind J.L.'s house. It was one of the last days of summer, a dry, lingering heat, and the fields around us had turned an exhausted shade of yellowish green.

I shook my head. I hadn't understood the question. The service had just ended, and I was watching Carl load snakes back into the bed of his truck.

"Me and Carolyn are going up there," Carl said. He hoisted a serpent box onto the tailgate and then slid it into the bed. Inside the box was a velvet-tailed timber rattler that he and Charles McGlocklin had both handled during the service that afternoon.

"Charles and Aline are going, too," he said, "if she can get off work." Carl lifted the tailgate and secured it while a trio of curious children from J.L.'s neighborhood tried to peer into the boxes.

"It's a ten-hour drive," he said to me, "but we like to take our time going up. You and Jim and Melissa ought to come."

That's when I remembered Jolo was in West Virginia. There was a famous snake-handling church there.

"I don't know," I said. "When is it?"

"Labor Day weekend. It's their twentieth annual home-coming. You'll miss some good services if you don't go," Carl said. "They always have a lot of serpents in Jolo." He stopped, smiled.

It had never come up between us before, but I knew what was on the tip of his tongue: Maybe I'd take up a serpent in Jolo. It made me wonder why he'd want me to. What would be in it for him if I did?

On the Friday of that Labor Day weekend, Jim, Melissa, and I left Birmingham in a driving rainstorm, the spent fury of Hurricane Andrew. It rained all the way to West Virginia, except for a spot in East Tennessee, where the clouds lifted momentarily to reveal the high green walls of the Appala-chians. These mountains aren't as raw and angular as the Rockies, or as mystical and remote as the Cascades. Instead, they seem mannered and familiar, predictable in the way they roll westward in alternating ridges and valleys. But in East Tennessee, the Appalachians converge in a chaos of intersecting planes. There, the mountains still look as wild and formidable as they must have to the first Europeans who entered the New World — entered it only, in ways, to become lost in it.

In preparation for our trip to Jolo, I'd read David Hackett Fischer's remarkable book *Albion's Seed,* a treatise on pat-

terns of immigration to America from the British Isles. I had it
in mind that in going back up the spine of the Appalachians
toward Jolo, I'd be retracing the route the snake handlers'
ancestors had taken as they descended toward Alabama. I
had not yet come to understand that these were my ancestors
too.

Fischer says that most of the immigrants who settled the
Appalachians arrived in waves from North Britain during the
middle of the eighteenth century. Predominantly Protestant
and poor, many of them had migrated first to Ireland, where
they felt trapped between the contempt of their own church
hierarchy and the hostility of Ireland's Catholic majority. But
unlike some of the earlier immigrants to America, the Scotch-
Irish, or Anglo-Irish, as they sometimes preferred to be
called, were not fleeing religious persecution. Instead, their
motives were primarily economic, a reaction to high rents,
low wages, and scarcity of food. Their flight to America,
though, suggested biblical themes.

*"On Jordan's stormy banks I stand and cast a wishful
eye,"* they would sing, *"to Canaan's fair and happy land
where my possessions lie. I am bound for the promised land,
I am bound for the promised land, oh who will come and go
with me? I am bound for the promised land."*

That they survived the ocean crossing was itself a triumph,
for the mortality rate during such ventures approached that

of the slave trade. Like most new arrivals, the survivors faced discrimination because of their relative poverty and their odd appearance and behavior. The Scotch-Irish had a reputation for being noisy, quarrelsome, and proud. They were easy targets for ridicule in the streets of Philadelphia and the other eastern seaports where they first disembarked. The men, lean and angular, dressed in sackcloth shirts and baggy pants. They stood out among the neatly dressed Quakers in leather breeches and carefully cut doublets. The young Scotch-Irish women were equally inappropriate in their tight-waisted skirts, openly sensual by some accounts. The Quaker women wore handkerchiefs to cover their bodices.

The Scotch-Irish were encouraged by the more sedate Quakers to seek land on the western frontier, and after the coldness and clamor of the cities, the new immigrants, with names like Rutherford, Graham, Armstrong, and Bankhead, must have ached for familiar terrain, places like the Shenandoah Valley of Virginia, or the Sequatchie and Grasshopper Valleys of Tennessee: long, sheltered valleys between hills with rocky outcroppings, settings that might remind them of the starkly beautiful border regions they had left behind in southern Scotland and northern England. The climate here would be temperate, the water plentiful, and once the trees had been cleared, the land might roll beneath their feet as it had in the shadows of the Cheviot Hills. But to get to these interior valleys, the immigrants had to cross the mountains, a journey with dangers we are unable to fully appreciate now.

Fortunately, these were a people accustomed to privation and sudden violence. Fischer says their heritage as border dwellers had turned them into tight-knit warrior clans that feuded endlessly over matters of real or perceived violations of honor. In their homeland, leadership had been bestowed on those with the strength and cunning to enforce it. Other forms of authority were rejected, whether from the local landowner, the state, or the church, so that even minor theological disputes became occasions for war. A particularly bloody rebellion was waged by an anticlerical Presbyterian sect called Cameronians, after their leader, Richard Cameron. Unable to defeat the Cameronians in battle, the British authorities eventually made use of their temperaments by enlisting them in the army to fight against Roman Catholics in the Scottish Highlands.

Not surprisingly, says Fischer, the culture that arose in the Appalachian mountains resurrected the character of that life along the border between Scotland and England. The Scotch-Irish had brought few material possessions with them, but they did bring their feuds, their language, and their love of music, strong drink, and sexual adventure. They also brought their fear of outsiders and their hostility toward clerics and established religions. Their own brand of Anglicanism or Presbyterianism would have seemed peculiar in the population centers of the Atlantic seaboard, but it was appropriate for life on the frontier. They sometimes called themselves People of the New Light, to distance themselves from the formalities and rigidity of Calvinism. The established churches emphasized good works or election as the means of salvation. But the New Lights celebrated what they called "free grace" and often worshiped outdoors under the stars, a practice that would culminate in the phenomenon of Cane Ridge.

The rigors of mountain life came to suit the Scotch-Irish, and instead of coming out of the mountains into the fertile valleys, many of the new settlers stayed, eking out a subsistence from the thin soil of the highland slopes. They grew their own produce and slaughtered their own livestock. They built their own cabins and furniture. They wove their own clothes, made their own whiskey. They were poor but self-sufficient. And although most, by the beginning of the twentieth century, had been lured into the coal fields, the mill towns of the Piedmont, or the industrial cities of the Midwest, many never found their way out of the mountains, or found their way out too late to apprehend the culture that had grown up in the promised land around them. Shortly after the turn of the twentieth century, these descendants of fierce Scotch-Irish immigrants awoke from their sojourn in the mountains to face the bitter reality of an industrialized and secularized society. Their sense of purposeful labor was eroded in the mines and factories. Their formerly close-knit families fractured. And they confronted a largely urban culture that appeared to have lost its concept of the sacred. The hill people had awoken to discover that the new Eden they'd inherited was doomed — mechanized and despoiled beyond recognition — and that they were lost in the very heart of it.

All along the highways through Tennessee and southwest Virginia, the signs were everywhere: Crazy Joe's Fireworks, Jack Daniel's whiskey, drag racing, turkey shoots, and barbecue. The South they suggested was straight out of the movies — idiosyncratic, lazy, restless, and self-absorbed. And that was what Jim and Melissa and I talked about on the drive, the discrepancy between the South of the popular imagination and the one we lived and worked in every day. But once the road narrowed and entered the mountains, the signs disappeared, replaced by mine tipples, mantrips, and long lines of train cars filled with coal that steamed in the rain. The last motels and hospital were at Grundy, Virginia, a mining town on the lip of a winding river between mountains so steep and irrational, they must have blocked most of the sun most of the day. It is difficult to imagine how children can grow up in such a place without carrying narrowed horizons into the rest of their lives.

But Grundy was an oasis compared with the country
between it and Jolo. Jim had taken the wheel on that stretch,
and I was able to see the landscape for what it was. The
topography was like a crumpled sheet of tin. And in that driving rain, at night, the road without guardrails seemed to be
a metaphor for our condition. We were barreling down a
rain-slick mountain after ten hours solid on the road, and the
safe haven at the end of our journey was a place where
strangers would be picking up rattlesnakes and drinking
strychnine out of mason jars. We wondered if we'd lost our
minds. Despite the fact that all three of us love danger, this
was a little much. Plus, we were lost. When we finally came
out of the mountains, we stopped at the first frame meeting
house with a crowd. It sounded Holiness from the outside,
all light and hubbub and an amplified nasal voice, but when
I got out of the van to investigate, I discovered that it was
simply a Friday night auction and Bingo game. I asked a
table of players near the open door if they knew where I
could find a snake-handling church.

"A *what?*" asked a woman in a United Mine Workers
sweatshirt. The others at her table glanced up in alarm, and I
got back in the van.

Farther on down the road, we found a man at a gas station who had heard of the church and could give us general
directions. His name, Doyle, was stitched on his shirt pocket,
and his forearm sported a tattoo of a sea monster. "Before

you cross the bridge, take a right," he told us. "You'll see it up the road a ways. I wouldn't get near those snakes if I were you."

Doyle's directions were so vague that we missed the church on the first pass, but saw it doubling back, a small frame building perched on the edge of a ravine.

We parked and got out.

It was still drizzling. The door of the church was open. Yellow light poured out onto the parked cars. The sanctuary had paneled walls and ceiling fans. Gravel crunched under our feet as we passed a dark man in a late-model car. He cupped his hand to light a cigarette. Near the front door of the church we could see the rusted remains of a car that lay suspended just over the edge of the ravine in a net of kudzu and sweet gum.

Inside the church, the air smelled of camphor and damp wool. Nobody in the congregation looked back at us, and I didn't see anyone I recognized right off the bat. There was no sign yet of Charles and Aline. A few other photographers were present, though, so Jim and Melissa found seats near them and got their cameras ready. But just before I sat down, on a pew three away from the front, I saw Carl Porter at the front, far right. I caught Carl's eye, and when he smiled, his glasses glinted in the overhead lights. Carolyn wasn't beside him, so I looked around the sanctuary until I saw her near the back. She nodded and waved. Her red hair had been cut and styled, and she was wearing a high-necked dress trimmed in lace. Carolyn didn't handle often, but when she did, it was with frightful abandon. At the last homecoming at Carl's church in Georgia, the snakes had been piled up on the pulpit. Carolyn picked up the entire pile. A rattlesnake struck at her and missed, but it was not so much the close call as Carolyn's reckless passion that unnerved us. Red hair flying, speaking in tongues, she had lifted up the pile of snakes to eye level and shouted at them until her face turned crimson, and then she had dropped them back onto the pulpit with such force that Carl had to come over and straighten them up.

Jim leaned over the back of the pew in front of me. "Looks like we missed the snakes," he whispered. He sounded disappointed. Like me, he'd become obsessed with the handlers. (On the way to Jolo, he'd talked about an art installation he wanted to do — a rusted-out car on blocks, with rattlesnakes coming out of its rotted front seat and Brother Carl preaching on the radio.) It's hard to know what to wish for in a serpent-handling church. You want to see the snakes taken out, but at the same time you don't. The more the snakes are taken out, the more the odds begin to work against the handlers. As an observer, you are in a moral quandary, responsible in an acute way for the wishes you make.

Four serpent boxes lay askew on a raised platform at the front, where a marionette of a man with thick glasses and the remains of a pompadour was flailing his arms in mid-sermon. "People today, they're hunting for an excuse," he said. "They want to look around and see what the other fellow's doing. They say, 'Well, I'm not doing this,' and 'I ain't gonna do that.'" He marched to one side of the platform in mock disgust. "Honey, I'll tell you what," he said. "You get the other fellow in your eye, and you'll both go to hell!" And then he hopped back across the platform on one foot while the congregation amened.

The preacher's name was Bob Elkins. A former mine superintendent, he was the official pastor of the church, which was called the Church of the Lord Jesus, but I would later find out that his wife, Sister Barbara Elkins, held true power. Sister Barbara was reportedly the last person still alive who had handled with George Went Hensley, the man legend said was the first to get the notion to take up a serpent, near Sale Creek, Tennessee, around 1910. At the time of our visit, Sister Barbara was seventy-six and so ill she couldn't attend the Friday night service. But she would be there on Saturday, as I would find out when I felt the sting of her reprimand.

As Brother Elkins brought his sermon to a close, Charles and Aline McGlocklin finally walked in. Brother Elkins pushed his glasses up onto his nose to get a good look at the couple, and then he continued preaching. Aline was wearing a satiny blue dress, and both she and Charles were spangled with droplets of rain. They sat next to Sister Carolyn.

When Brother Elkins had finished, Charles took to the

platform with his guitar. I assumed that Brother Carl, the visiting evangelist for this year's homecoming, had invited Charles to sing and preach a little. Sermons at snake-handling churches are short but numerous. Nobody ever uses notes, preferring to let the Spirit move. Charles was a master of this kind of improvisation, but that night was his first visit to Jolo, and he seemed nervous. The West Virginia crowd was a hard-looking lot, stricter in dress and behavior than congregations farther South. Hand-printed signs on the wall behind the pulpit forbade such things as short hair on women, long hair or beards or mustaches on men, short sleeves on either sex, and gossip, talebearing, lying, backbiting, and bad language from the pulpit. The West Virginians had been in this thing a long time, and they'd been hurt. The year before, one of their members, Ray Johnson, had died after being bit by a rattlesnake during a service at the church. His son-in-law, Jeffrey Hagerman, a new member, had been bitten four times. Barbara Elkins's own daughter, Columbia, had died of snakebite at the church in 1961, and Barbara's son, Dewey Chafin — a handsome, disabled coal miner with broad shoulders and white hair — had been bitten 116 times.

Charles had been bitten only once, and that was when he saw a rattlesnake crossing the road in Alabama and picked it up to impress some fellows he worked with. "They were sinner men," Aline confided. Charles maintained that the bite didn't even hurt him. The dilemma was clear: Charles hadn't been hurt, and now he was fixing to preach to a bunch of strangers, at their own homecoming, who *had* been hurt, and hurt bad.

"The Bible says the Holy Ghost will lead you, teach you, and guide you," he said. "I didn't even have a map to show me this place." Despite his smile, he was greeted with silence. "I know we drove about five hundred miles to get here," he continued.

Still, nobody said anything. Charles strummed a chord on his guitar and looked out over the congregation as if waiting for the right words to come. He had, after all, seen angels and been taken out in the spirit for long messages from the Lord. "You know, there's a lot of church forms and a lot of church buildings, but there ain't but one church," he said, and that seemed to start the crowd warming to him. They knew what would follow. "There ain't but one God," Charles said. "One church."

Amen.

"One God, one Lord, one faith, one baptism, one father and God of all who is above all, and over all, and in you all!"

Amen. Yes, he had them.

"And it's time the people that's in the real church of the living God, the one that Jesus gave Peter the keys to the kingdom to in the sixteenth chapter of the book of Matthew, it's time that God's people let the world know God's the same yesterday, today, and forever!"

Amen. Thank God.

"Amen," he said back to them in relief. "That's already been worth the trip."

He had hit them with the Holiness precepts: one God, one spirit, the alpha and omega, unchanging. He did not say it then, but everyone understood what rightly followed: God had but one name, Jesus. For the church at Jolo, no matter how it differed otherwise from the churches in Alabama and Georgia, was a Jesus Name church. Instead of baptizing in the name of the Father, Son, and Holy Ghost, they baptized in the name of Jesus. To them, Jesus *was* the name of the Father, Son, and Holy Ghost. Trinitarians called them "Jesus Onlys." They called Trinitarians "three-God people."

Charles McGlocklin had staked his claim with the West Virginians as a Jesus Only like them, and riding their approval, he picked up his guitar again and started singing a song called "Like a Prodigal Son." He was accompanied on bass guitar by Dewey Chafin, on drums by Kirby Hollins, and on organ by Kirby's wife, Lydia Elkins Hollins, the granddaughter of matriarch Barbara Elkins and daughter of Columbia, who had died of snakebite in this very sanctuary while she was in her early twenties. Charles strode back and forth across the platform as he sang. *"Well, I want to go home, and feast with the Father. The table is set, and they're waiting for me. . . ."*

The members of the congregation stood and swayed to the

music, a gentle hill ballad that suddenly took, with Lydia Hollins's eccentric organ work, a dark and dissonant turn. Lydia, head cocked, seemed to be searching intently for an unexplored harmonic. Dewey Chafin, on bass, flicked his wrist spasmodically, just shy of the beat. The effect was gradual, an elevation. I felt myself moved in an unexpected way, as though the music were a mild intoxicant. Most of us had tambourines, including Brother Timmy McCoy, a red-haired man who worked in produce at the Kroger's in Richlands, Virginia. Brother Timmy was dressed in a ruffled yellow shirt, vest, and pointed shoes — the Liberace of snake handling, I thought. He threw his head back as he shook his tambourine. The light in the church seemed to have changed. It was softer, more liquid. Behind us, Aline lifted her hands into the air, reaching for the Spirit, like she had at the brush-arbor meetings. Her eyelids were closed, her fingers extended in a curiously splayed pattern that suggested desire in the process of being remedied. I felt gooseflesh on my arms as I watched her, and Melissa unobtrusively started taking photographs of her.

When Brother Charles finished his song and stepped down from the platform, it was clear he had been a success. He had invoked the Spirit and set the stage for Brother Carl, an old friend to the believers at the Church of the Lord Jesus. In typical fashion, Brother Carl seemed to be hanging back.

Maybe it was modesty. Maybe he was just waiting on the Spirit. When he finally did take the platform, he was holding his Bible close. "This thing is good," he said. And by *thing,* he meant it all — the Bible, the serpent handling, the way of Holiness, the Holy Ghost. "It'll make you talk in the unknown tongue," he said. "My daddy used to say, if you want to see the devil run, shoot him in the back with the Holiness gun." And he held his Bible aloft. "This is it right here. With the word of God, you can put that devil to flight! That's what Jesus used to get the devil when he was fasting for forty days and nights. He used the Word!" *Amen. Thank God.* "He'll put the devil to *flight.* It'll make him put his tail between his legs and run like a scalded dog!" And he hopped and convulsed like it was him instead of the dog who'd been hit with the Holiness gun. "This thing is real!" *Amen. Thank God.*

"It takes the Spirit of God!" Brother Carl shouted. "They say this thing just started in George Hensley's day. Well, honey, I want you to know this thing's been around for years and years, when Moses built that graven serpent, and they looked upon it and lived! There's a hedge," he said, and he threw his arms out as though to describe its arc. "That hedge is Jesus!"

Amen. Thank God.

"And let me tell you, if we break that hedge, we'll get serpent bit!" He was pointing straight into the congregation now, crouched and red-faced. "You can leave this world, and honey, it don't take you long to do it!"

Amen. They knew how long it'd take.

Carl finished with a flourish. "We better know who our Saviour is!"

Oh, yes! they said. *We do!*

I was sweating and expectant, lifted on the general surge. I could tell something was about to break loose, but I couldn't predict its shape or form. I just knew that I was going to be part of it, and during the next song, "Everything's Gonna Be All Right," things started getting a little wild. Lydia Hollins was singing in a voice as raw and tortured as Janis Joplin's when flamboyant Brother Timmy, suddenly seized by the rhythm of the music, started dancing down the aisle toward the front, his tambourine going. I'd seen him in white patent leather shoes and a powder blue shirt with ruffles at the homecoming at Carl's church in May. Timmy had whirled in circles like a dervish, a rattlesnake in each hand. This time, though, he didn't head immediately for the serpent boxes. He just danced in front of the platform, stomping his feet and tossing his head in a step reminiscent of that old 1960s routine called The Pony.

"Everything's gonna be all right." Close on his heels came an older couple, Ray McAllister and his wife, Gracie, a woman in a simple pink jersey and flower-print skirt, her

gray hair pinned in a bun. She seemed the least likely person in the world to pick up a rattlesnake, but in the midst of her dancing, she suddenly veered toward one of the serpent boxes. Unclasping its lid, she took out a two-and-a-half-foot-long canebrake rattlesnake and held it up with both hands. Then she turned a slow circle with the snake outstretched, her face transfigured by something like pain or remorse.

It occurred to me then that seeing a handler in the ecstasy of an anointing is not like seeing religious ecstasy at all. The expression seems to have more to do with Eros than with God, in the same way that sex often seems to have more to do with death than with pleasure. The similarity is more than coincidence, I thought. In both sexual and religious ecstasy, the first thing that goes is self. The entrance into ecstasy is surrender. Handlers talk about *receiving* the Holy Ghost. But when the Holy Ghost is fully come upon someone like Gracie McAllister, the expression on her face reads exactly the opposite — as though someone, or something, were being violently taken away from her. The paradox of Christianity, one of many of which Jesus speaks, is that only in losing ourselves do we find ourselves, and perhaps that's why photos of the handlers so often seem to be portraits of loss.

By the time Gracie had passed the snake to her husband, Ray, a half dozen more of the faithful had joined them and had begun lifting snakes from the other boxes in no apparent order and with no apparent plan. They were shouting praise or praying out loud. Some were speaking in tongues. Things were beginning to spiral out of control. I came to the front then, banging my tambourine against my leg. I'd never been able to stay away from the center of storms. Brother Carl smiled at me. He was holding up a four-foot black timber rattler. He held it with reverence and a certain tenderness. I saw him stroke its chin. To my left, Dewey Chafin, the white-haired ex–coal miner, took up three rattlesnakes at the same time. He dropped one onto the floor in the confusion, and stooped to pick it back up. One of his thumbs was still bandaged from a copperhead bite he'd received a few weeks before. A few feet away from Dewey, young Jeffrey Hagerman, twenty-five, the son-in-law of the last member to die of snakebite, grasped a rattlesnake in either hand and hopped joyfully with them while his wide-eyed children, one in pajamas, watched from a nearby pew. *"Everything's gonna be all right."* Then the men passed the snakes among themselves. At one point, all six snakes wound up with Brother Charles, who was standing next to me. *"Everything's gonna be all right."* With one of his massive hands, Charles held the snakes in a row by their tails, and smoothed them out with his other, as though he were straightening a rack of ties. I thought my eyes were playing tricks on me. The rattlesnakes seemed to have turned to rubber or gauze.

For twenty minutes, we continued to dance and sing, while
the music ground on like some wacko, amphetamine dirge.
Sister Lydia's voice was like cloth ripping. *"Everything's
gonna be all right."* Sure it is, I thought. At one point Dewey
Chafin gathered all six rattlesnakes together and held them
up with one hand. Then Brother Carl took the rattlesnakes
and put them on top of his head before distributing them
back to the other men. The action was so wild and fast, I lost
track of where the snakes were or who had them. I didn't
care. Brother Timmy careened into me, his rattlesnake in my
face. I caught a glimpse of Jim and his camera tumbling
backward under Timmy's feet. Melissa was on her knees trying to get photos of the snakes from beneath. The Holy Ghost
had descended like a hurricane, and we were all in danger of
being swept away. But right at that moment when it seemed
the frenzy couldn't restrain itself any longer, the lunatic music
stopped, and everything seemed to go into slow motion. We'd
reached the eye of the storm now. It was absolutely calm.
The brothers and sisters continued to cradle the snakes as
they prayed or spoke in tongues. Sister Lydia came from
behind the electric organ and got herself a copperhead to
stroke. The air seemed brighter than it had been before.
Soothing. Clarifying. It was as though a thin, light oil had
been poured down on us all.

I'd had this feeling before, under fire, in El Salvador. It was
an adrenaline rush. I felt as though I were in an element

other than air. The people around me were illuminated.
Their faces were filled with light. And it seemed as though
nothing could happen to any of us that would harm us,
although in retrospect, of course, I knew that not to be the
case. We felt invulnerable, forever alive. But then the music
intruded again, slower, more stately this time, and without
any other audible signal, the handlers started returning the
snakes to their boxes. They actually stood in line, waiting
their turn to guide the serpents back into the flat cages with
"Jesus Saves" carved in the sides. After all of the serpents
were safely inside, and the brothers had laid hands on Gracie
McAllister to heal her troubled heart, I was seized by the
desire to testify. It was an imperative. I seemed to have no
control over my legs or my mouth. I stalked out in front of
the congregation, and in what sounded to me like an unnatu-
rally loud and guttural voice, announced that the Holy Ghost
had led me to West Virginia to document these events in
order that the gospel might be spread all over the country. I
said it as though these were fighting words and I were daring
anybody to disagree. I was astonished at myself afterward.
Appalled is not too strong a word. At the moment, though,
the words not only seemed right, but inevitable.

"This thing is real!" I told Brother Carl after the service. I
was sweaty and ebullient.

"That's right," Carl said, pounding me on the back and

looking sideways into my face, inquisitively, the way a physi-
cian studies a patient's eyes to see how the pupils are respond-
ing to light.

My most common nightmare is of having to go to the bathroom, but not being able to find one. So I wind up doing it
in public, squatting on a busy street corner or in the center
of the living room at a party, and I wake up utterly humiliated.
Shame seems to drive my psychic engine. I don't know why
this is so. All I know is that I am excessively calculating,
especially when I appear not to be, in order to avoid being
shamed. Early on, I learned to feign spontaneity. During my
drinking days, I honed it to an art. But what happened that
Friday night in Jolo wasn't calculated. I had experienced
something genuine, and I was awed by what I had seen. I
might as well have been watching people defy the law of
gravity or breathe underwater. It was that startling, that
inexplicable.

Jim and Melissa felt the same way. The mood in the van on
the way back to our motel in Virginia was one of reckless
exhilaration. Jim and I had seen similar displays of snake
handling at the homecoming at Carl's church in Kingston,
but not this close up. The handling Melissa had seen before
had been nothing like this. She was duly impressed, although
she confided that the snakes did not interest her as much as

they did us. Maybe the snakes were a male thing, she suggested, although plenty of women do handle them. But what obsessed Melissa was Aline reaching for the Spirit. I'd forgotten about Aline during the chaos of the handling. Had she handled that night? No, Melissa said.

Whenever Jim and I had talked about the handling in the past, he would always suggest that there was a technique to it. Most of the time, the handlers held the snakes very lightly, right in the middle, about the place where you'd lift them up with a snake hook. The snakes seem balanced like that, and unable to strike. But tonight blew that theory. The handlers just grabbed them any old way they could and were doing whatever they wanted to them.

We posed all kinds of questions to one another: Why didn't anybody get bit? Maybe the loud music disorients the snakes? *Snakes don't have ears.* But they must be able to feel the vibrations. *What about all the times there wasn't any music, and everything was still?* I had been to scores of services by now. Something extraordinary had happened tonight. Jim and Melissa agreed, a sort of group hypnosis, group hysteria. "Of course, it could also have had something to do with" — and here I paused, not because I knew how Jim and Melissa would take this, but because I, too, was surprised by my thinking it — "the presence of the Holy Ghost."

Jim looked at me. "That's what I thought you'd say."

. . .

The rain stopped completely sometime during the night. The next morning started off cool and bright, but by afternoon the last of the summer heat had returned. The air stayed clear, though, as fine as glass, and that evening when we drove up to the church again for the Saturday night service, the light through the trees was low and red.

The crowd was larger that second night. There were many more members of the press there, among them a television crew from North Carolina who had shown up with their blinding lights and impeccably dressed Asian-American anchorwoman. Her suit was gray flannel, her hair perfectly in place. She was poised and articulate in front of the camera, but she didn't seem to have a clue about what was going on in the church itself.

Sister Barbara Elkins, the ailing matriarch, had shown up with a fruit jar of strychnine solution. She had mixed it herself. "She mixes it strong," Jeff Hagerman said to me. "If you get scared or get your mind off God, you start to feel it." Throughout most of the service, Sister Barb sat behind the pulpit with her handkerchief to her head. She was a large, flaccid woman in a black shift. She seemed to be in enormous pain. Her husband, Brother Bob, preached awhile, as did visiting pastors from neighboring states. When the snakes came out, the handling seemed a bit less spontaneous than it had the night before. Maybe it was the television crew's lights, maybe the presence of Sister Barb. I was at the front with the handlers, as I had been the previous night, when Brother Bob suddenly unscrewed the lid of the fruit jar on the pulpit and took a few swigs. He wiped his mouth on his sleeve and handed the jar down to Jeff Hagerman, who did the same. After drinking from the jar, Jeff shook his head and then started whirling with his arms outstretched, faster and faster, while he clicked his heels on the hard wooden floor. *Bless him!* someone said. *Give him victory!* said someone else. The music mounted higher. Jeff threw back his head and howled like an animal in heat. Then he careened out of his whirling dance and staggered to a nearby pew. He was smiling. He was fine, just dizzy, and the congregation erupted in amens and thank Gods.

Sister Barb stood on unsteady feet, and Brother Bob handed her the microphone. She started at one end of the platform and worked her way down. She was wincing in pain, but there was something she wanted to make clear. She'd had it with outsiders in the midst of the handlers, and she had a few words to say about the subject: "These reporters need to stay back. This up here is for the saints of God. And it's not a show. It's for people that worship God." She emphasized each word with a flick of her handkerchief. "We're not a hateful people, we're not haughty people, but these reporters, if they want to make their money, can make it back there and not up here where they endanger people's lives."

Sister Barbara walked back behind the pulpit, occasionally touching her handkerchief to her temple. Brother Timmy and his wife gave her an amen, but most of the other handlers were silent. I felt my own face flush as I realized she was talking most particularly about me.

"I've been in this little better than fifty years," she said. "I've been bit about sixteen times. It was the making of me. But I know you go down in the jaws of death. Just about all of us here that handle serpents has come to that point." She leaned into the pulpit for support. "I hope I make it. I hope we're saved." It was not rhetorical. She seemed to understand her time was short, and that she and the other handlers had better have chosen the right way. "There's more to it than handling serpents, anyhow," she said. "They come to get pictures of serpents, but you know there's more to it."

I knew that full well, but the idea seemed fresh to her. It seemed to rouse her. She brought herself up to full height and stepped back from the pulpit. "I know *my* blessing was handling serpents," she said with dignity. "Handling fire. But they was other things that went with it."

Yes there was. Amen.

"God don't play games," she said.

No, he don't.

"And if he sent me to you, I don't care what was wrong with you, you'll be healed."

Thank God.

"I just love God's people," she said. "I'm glad some of my children turned out. I noticed one of my grandsons by marriage, he had enough respect; he wanted the pictures for his own use and he stayed back."

Yes, he did.

"You know you can dishonor God."

Amen. You sure can.

She was looking straight at me, but I held her gaze. Her eyes were flat, reptilian.

For most of the rest of the service, I stayed behind an imaginary line with the other journalists. When I stepped outside later for some fresh air, I could see the mountains clearly, great black silhouettes against the sharp-edged sky. The sight of them stirred something like homesickness in me. But if it was homesickness, it was for a place I'd never been. Brother Carl had followed me out. He hugged me and said, "I knew she was talking about you. I should have come to your defense. I'm sorry."

I assured him it was all right, that I understood. Besides, my mind was somewhere else by then. The rain had moved on through the valley we were in, and the moon was visible through some high, gauzy clouds. Carl went back inside the church. As I stood in the dark outside, listening to the cicadas and the tambourines, I wondered about those border dwellers who had sailed for the promised land two hundred years before, in search of a new Eden. I thought about them finding their way through these mountains, the People of the New Light. I wondered whether they'd crossed the mountains around here somewhere, or farther south at the Cumberland Gap or Saluda Gap, or even farther still, at the great bend in the Tennessee River near Chattanooga, where the states of Alabama, Tennessee, and Georgia meet, and the last great plateau of the Appalachians, Sand Mountain, begins its dead aim straight for the furnaces of Birmingham.

When I finally went back inside the church, my mind was still lingering on the mountains and the clouds that nearly hid the moon, but when I saw what was happening at the front of the sanctuary, my heart nearly turned in my chest. Aline McGlocklin had left her seat in the middle of the congregation and was standing near the front, exactly as she had stood under the brush arbor on Sand Mountain. Her hands were raised, her face upturned. Her lower jaw was trembling, and I imagined the sound before I heard it: "Akiii, akiii, akiii. . . ." In front of Aline stood her husband Charles, with the four-foot black timber rattlesnake outstretched in his hands. He was getting ready to hand it to her.

The rattlesnake was so big Charles could hardly get a hand around it. He would later tell me that the Lord spoke to him in that moment and asked him, "Who do you love more, me or your wife?" Charles said the answer was God, and so he decided to go ahead and give her the snake. It was a moment that suggested that most ancient of stories — a garden, a serpent, a man and his wife. But now the story seemed oddly reversed, as though by giving his wife the serpent, the man could restore the communion with God that had been broken. Aline's hands, which had been stretched upward, now suddenly turned to receive. But as Charles began to hand the rattlesnake to her, it rolled. He steadied it. It rolled again, doing a full turn in his hands, as though it were on a lathe. Charles stepped back and handed the serpent to Carl Porter, who prayed over it aloud before he stepped forward and lay it into Aline's hands. Her face changed. It seemed to open out. The sound that she made did not resemble human speech. *Have your way, Lord,* someone said as Aline trembled in ecstasy with the big black rattlesnake outstretched in her hands. I was only an observer, but I felt I had been drawn into something so painfully intimate that I was morally obliged to look away even as I stared the harder. I wanted to step in and rescue Aline, but from what? Wasn't it the same thing that was happening to me?

6
ROOTS

An hour before sundown we reached another barren region inhabited by "poor white trash." Their houses were of the worst imaginable description, and how they managed to obtain a living upon such a soil, was a problem to us. Yet hither the pitiless monopoly of the slaveholding class had driven them, and, by some means or other, they manage to wring sufficient food to keep themselves and their children from starving, out of these inhospitable rocks.

— dispatch from The New York Times *dated April 14, 1862, "Advance into Alabama"*

Right before he died, my father got interested in genealogy. "As far as I know," he said, "no Covington has ever left anything to anybody, and I'm not going to be the one to break the tradition." Dad meant it as a joke. He had already given me the best gifts — unqualified love, a moral education, and a good name. But there were three tangibles that he left as well. Before his death he deeded me two and a half acres of palmetto scrubland in central Florida, fifty miles south of Orlando. It was part of a massive real estate venture that had turned belly-up, the largest bankruptcy in the history of the state. River Ranch Acres, it had been called. *Ranch,* because it wasn't on the coast. *River,* because there was supposed to be one nearby. The sales literature had been filled with drawings of horses and cattle. But the development had no roads, no power, no water. The plots hadn't even been surveyed. My dad bought the two and a half acres anyway, as an investment, he said, the only investment he had ever made. But I think he really bought the land because he had always loved Westerns. His favorite movie was *Gunfight at the O.K. Corral.*

The second thing Dad left was a wooden cigar box that had belonged to my grandfather Covington. In it were a straight razor, two shaving brushes still caked with dried lather, my father's tortoiseshell pocketknife, and a few yellowing buttons.

The third thing Dad left me was a green binder containing what little family research he'd been able to do before his lungs gave out. I couldn't bear to look at it, the spidery handwriting on green ledger paper, done in pencil in case of mistakes. My father had been a supervisor in the production planning department at Tennessee Coal and Iron. His responsibilities included seeing to it that Continental Can received the exact quantity of tin they had been promised, and on time. He was, therefore, a perfectionist. Decades after his office moved to a hill overlooking the mills, he continued to get his hair cut by the same black barber downtown because the man always remembered, without having to be asked, to clip the hairs in his nose. The records Dad kept on his 1977

Aunt Daisy, the prophetess

© JIM NEEL

Glenn Summerford

J.L. Dyal, Charles McGlocklin, and Carl Porter

The legendary Punkin Brown (left)

"Spread the word! We're coming down from the mountains!"
Brother Bob Stanley

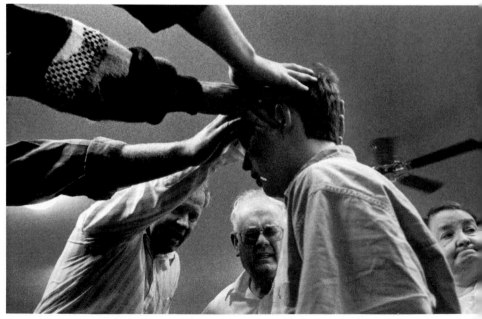

The laying on of hands

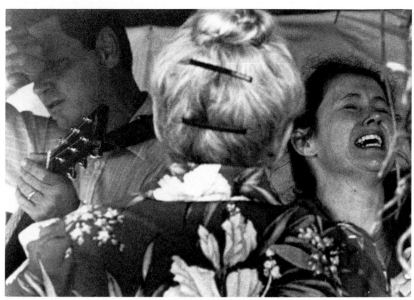

Charles and Aline McGlocklin

"We'd better put our house in order!"
Charles McGlocklin, the End-Time Evangelist

Handler Rayford Dunn

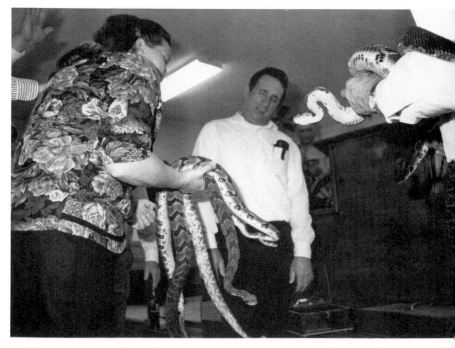

Bobbie Sue Thompson and Billy Summerford

Dewey Chafin

Dozier Edmonds

The healing of Gracie McAllister

Aline McGlocklin

orange Astre station wagon included the original car dealer-
ship's ad cut neatly from the paper. He had kept that ad for
nearly twelve years. At the time of his death, he had the war-
ranties for every electrical device, including can openers and
toasters, that he and my mother had ever purchased, arranged
in labeled envelopes. It broke my heart to open the green
binder and see him hard at work again, trying to get one last
record straight.

I can tell you the exact moment I decided to take a closer
look at the binder. It was New Year's Eve, 1992, at the Church
of the Lord Jesus Christ in Kingston, Georgia, Brother Carl
Porter's church. We were attending an all-night watch service,
complete with snake handling, Holy Communion, laying on
of hands, and chicken and egg salad sandwiches in the basement after we'd washed each other's feet.

We arrived in mid-service. The moment occurred when
the music got cranked up, and the snakes started coming out
of the boxes. Vicki had been to a snake-handling church
before, but this was the first time we'd brought our daughters, Ashley, then seven, and Laura, then five. We normally
took them everywhere we went, but I was a little nervous
this time. Our daughters are resilient and adventuresome. I
didn't want to press them too much, though.

Laura, like my mother, is an artist. She took one look at
Brother Junior McCormick dancing in front of the pulpit with

two rattlesnakes draped across his shoulders and decided to spend some time outside in the van, where she drew pictures of rattlesnakes and tambourines. Vicki and I took turns keeping her company. Ashley, though, was transfixed. It was a surprise to me. Physically, Ashley is a dead ringer for a Covington. She has the Covington long arms and the Covington chin. And like my father, she is a careful person —exact in her reckonings and stubborn in her defense of what she believes to be right. But she doesn't like to be startled, and she has no use for loud noises or extravagant gestures. I was afraid a serpent-handling service would be more than she could handle. But when the music started, she looked up at me wide eyed and grinning, and in no time she was clapping her hands and stomping her feet. The snakes didn't seem to faze her one bit. "Cool!" she exclaimed over the uproar. It was as though the shouting and the shrieking and the raw hillbilly music had been imprinted on her genes, like something deep within her she was remembering. I thought of this thing called cell memory. I thought of a part of her — an ancestor — resurrected, alive, caught by surprise.

The sight of my daughter, so clearly a Covington, so clearly at home in the chaos of a snake-handling service, made me quicken. *Were we actually kin to these people?* I was going to look more closely at my father's notes in the green binder. I wanted more. Who were my people? Who were my daughters kin to?

When the snakes had been put away, and the music had stopped, Vicki and Laura came back into the sanctuary. Brother Carl placed a bottle of Welch's Sparkling Concord Grape Juice on one side of the pulpit, where minutes before a rattlesnake had stretched. On the other side, he put a bottle of Manischewitz wine. Between them sat a pan of unleavened bread. And I knew we were going to have Communion.

It was the first time Carl had celebrated Communion in the new sanctuary, which was three years old. Rituals like Communion are rare events in snake-handling churches, anyway; snake handlers don't stand on ceremony or pay much attention to the traditional church calendar. I'd been in a snake-handling church on Easter morning when the word *Easter* was not even mentioned. But Carl's church seemed to be striving for a measure of respectability, and he wanted to make sure that if they did something like this, they did it right.

Carl opened his Bible to a passage in Matthew. *"And as they were eating,"* he read, *"Jesus took bread, and blessed it, and brake it, and gave it to the disciples, and said, Take, eat; this is my body."*

Carl looked up from the book. "Now, he didn't mean it was really his body."

Amen.

"They weren't cannibals."

Thank God.

"Can you imagine me taking a big bite of Brother Junior over there, and him not even cooked? He's forty something years old. He'd be tough as foot leather!"

Bless him, sweet Jesus!

Carl looked back at the book. *"And he took the cup,"* he read, *"and gave thanks, and gave it to them, saying, Drink ye all of it; For this is my blood of the new testament, which is shed for many for the remission of sins."*

Again, he glanced up. "I sure ain't gonna drink nobody's blood."

Amen.

"I ain't no vampire."

Praise God!

Carl solemnly closed his Bible and held it up in one hand. "This book here," he said, "will tell you everything you need to know. It'll tell you how to bake bread. It'll tell you how to raise a garden, how to treat your wife, how to wash your feet. It'll tell you how to comb your hair."

Then he blessed the grape juice, wine, and unleavened bread. A certain awkwardness descended on us all, but at Carl's encouragement everybody lined up either in front of the Welch's or in front of the Manischewitz. Vicki and the girls and I chose the grape juice. Charles and Aline McGlocklin chose the wine. Drinking unfermented grape juice, Charles confided, would be like taking up a nonpoisonous snake. Bill Pelfrey, another snake-handling preacher from Newnan, Georgia, helped Carl serve the Communion in Dixie cups. As each member of the congregation took his cup, he also reached into the pan for a piece of unleavened bread and popped it into his mouth. The women stepped off to the side to drink their grape juice or wine. The men threw theirs back right where they stood, then crumpled the cups and looked around for a trash can. Occasionally one of them would throw his arms out and praise God. Carl's cousin, Gene Sherbert, spoke rapidly in tongues.

It wasn't quite like the Communions I'd taken in my family's Methodist church in Birmingham. Back then, we went to the altar by pews and knelt. The organist played softly in the background. Brother Jack Dillard, in the black choir robe he wore only for this occasion, would serve the Welch's grape juice in tiny glasses arranged on a circular silver tray. The host, also served from a silver tray, consisted of crumbled-up Premium saltines. But except for those details, the spirit within the churches was not so different. We Methodists just didn't speak in tongues, and prior to Communion we didn't handle rattlesnakes.

After everybody in Brother Carl's church had been served, he held up his Bible and said, "It says here they ate his flesh and drunk his blood and sang a hymn and went out to the Mount of Olives."

So we sang a hymn, accompanied by guitars, drums, and Carl himself on cymbals, and then Junior McCormick and Gene Sherbert brought out pans and pitchers filled with water for the foot washing. I'd been waiting for this part. I'd heard of foot washing, but had never done it. I liked what it was supposed to represent — the idea of following Jesus by becoming a servant to others.

Carl put down his cymbals and got his Bible out again. *"If I then, your Lord and Master, have washed your feet; ye also ought to wash one another's feet."* Then he looked up. "I want the women to go downstairs now," he said. They would wash their feet in private. I watched the women file out. Vicki had dressed the girls in Holiness fashion, in modest, long dresses. Ashley's was teal-blue, Laura's ivory. Vicki had attempted to make herself plain, too, tossing aside her dangling earrings at the last moment. Once the women disappeared down the wooden stairs, the men gathered on the deacons' bench and began taking off their shoes and socks. Brother Carl didn't say anything.

The bare feet were gray and bruised looking in the fluorescent light. Most of the feet had thick yellow nails and crooked toes, rough heels, tufts of hair. I was a little apprehensive as I took off my shoes and socks and rolled up the legs of my jeans. I didn't want to go first, and was relieved I didn't have to. Brother Carl volunteered to do that. Junior

McCormick and Gene Sherbert sat on either side of him on the deacons' bench. When Carl put his feet into the pan of water, he also placed his hands on the shoulders of Junior and Gene as they leaned over to rub his feet and splash water against his legs. All the other men gathered around. It was like a rugby scrum. Everybody tried to get a hand in the water, which was slick with the olive oil Carl had poured in. Carl's head was thrown back, his eyes closed. "Lift him up, Lord," said Brother Bill Pelfrey.

I was sandwiched in between Brother Bill and Charles McGlocklin. They were jiggling against me as they stirred the water in the pan. Brother Bill stomped his foot twice. The keys he wore on a chain through his belt loop jangled. *"Ah-canna-helimos,"* he said. *"Co-taka-helican."*

"Thank God," Carl said.

"Yes, Jesus," said Brother Charles.

I groped around in the water. I felt Carl's ankle, his stiff toes, and the hands of the other men. It was peculiar and intimate to touch other men like that.

The men began praying out loud. The voices spiraled louder and faster.

"Thy will be done!" shouted Bill Pelfrey.

"We ask it in the name of Jesus!" echoed Brother Charles.

"Jesus!" shouted the other men.

"Sweet Jesus!" said a blond-haired boy with buck teeth.

Carl opened his eyes and looked at the boy with studied surprise, as though he were seeing him for the first time.

"Do you want to go next?" he asked.

The boy nodded. I don't know whose son he was, although I remembered seeing him earlier in the service with a large family Bible in his hand. Carl lifted his feet out of the water, and Gene Sherbert dried them off with a towel. Then Carl and the boy changed places.

The movement of the men changed now. They were more methodical, more delicate. During the washing, Bill Pelfrey offered up a long and intricate prayer that collapsed into tongues at intervals, like the breaking of a wave. I stepped back from the men and looked at the boy's face through their shoulders and heads. His shirt had miniature sailboats on it. His eyes were closed, his lips parted. His front teeth, one of which was chipped, glistened in the overhead light. And his body seemed to rock with the motion of the men's hands on his feet. I was moved by something I could not name. It was like desire, and not like desire, a longing for something that could not be possessed. It was what I felt sometimes when I looked in on my daughters sleeping and was suddenly aware that they were not merely bursts of restless energy and sound, but bodies, solid and temporal, that had been entrusted to me.

"You next?" Brother Charles asked me. I'd lost track of

what was going on. The boy had already moved to another spot on the bench, where one of the men was drying his feet.

I nodded and sat in the boy's place on the bench. When I put my feet into the water, I immediately felt the men's hands all over them. They were praying aloud and invoking the name of Jesus. Brother Carl put his hand on my head, and I felt a vibration move along it and into my scalp. But the washing of my own feet seemed anticlimactic. The heart of the experience was watching the boy's chipped tooth glisten as his feet were washed by men.

The next morning, when we got back to Birmingham, I took out my father's green binder, which had sat since his death in a bookcase underneath a stack of magazines and unanswered correspondence. Until then, I hadn't really felt a need to know where my people had come from. But there was something about the way Ashley had responded to the snake-handling service, the sight of her clapping her hands and stomping her feet, that convinced me we were connected in some way to a distinctive mountain culture. Ashley would write in her school journal: "Mother and Daddy took me to a snake-handling church for New Year's Eve. They had copperheads, rattlesnakes, tambourines, and we got our feet washed at midnight." Her teacher would casually bring the

journal out at a parent-teacher conference, and tilt her head as if to say, "And do you want to elaborate?"

I had grown up in the 1950s, with radio and television and *Reader's Digest,* and I had assumed that everyone around us was pretty much alike. The past didn't matter. The only history we knew was who we'd fought against in World War II. All we cared about was the present. And all our parents seemed to care about was the future.

East Lake was a solid neighborhood, just shy of middle class, with families trying to do things right, making sure that teeth got filled, shot records were up to date, church attendance pins got won, spelling words learned. Our parents were preparing us to do better than they had, as they had done better than their parents, but beyond that we had no idea who we were. All we knew was that wherever we came from, we didn't want to go back there.

My mother and her sister had been born in a rural crossroads town southeast of Birmingham, but their father had moved them in and out of the city numerous times, following rumors of work. They'd grown up poor in the mining camps of Jefferson County, where, for a time, my grandfather was a hired gun for the coal company. My mother remembers hiding in the cellar while striking miners broke out all their windows with bats. She and her sister found a dead man in their yard one time, no questions asked. They often went

hungry. Their mother, my grandmother Nellie Russell, washed coal dust off their clothes outdoors in a number-ten tub. She had never smoked in her life, but she wound up dying of emphysema anyway. My grandfather, Charlie Russell, the strike buster and eventual railroad detective, died in the state mental hospital of the syphilis he'd contracted riding the rails. For many years my mother kept his revolver in a wooden box on the top shelf of her closet. Before he got too sick, he and my grandmother had lived in a big rock house in Pinson, Alabama. But it was the mental hospital I remember best. We'd visit him on weekends, picnic on the grounds. I used to think of the gold-domed mental hospital as our equivalent of Tara.

My father had fared better as a child. His father, though, had been born in Summit, Alabama, a ridgetop west of Sand Mountain. Only one of my grandfather Covington's four siblings survived past adolescence. Her name was Tetie. She died in 1916, at the age of forty-six. She was the first of the children to be born in Alabama, which meant that the Covington family had come to the state sometime between 1862 and 1869. But exactly where the Covingtons began their journey, where they crossed the mountains, how they lived, what they believed, who they were, nobody knew. Nobody asked. The Covingtons were a people who'd left their pasts behind. A door had been shut somewhere.

Most of what my father had written in the green binder were the names, birthdays, wedding dates, and deaths of his eleven siblings and their children, a hefty enough task. The history of the family, though, was slim. Dad's paternal grandfather, Richard Covington, had been born somewhere in North Carolina around 1826 and had married a Mary Clark from South Carolina in 1858. Their oldest child, Anna, was born in 1860 in North Carolina. The family disappeared after that and reappeared in the 1880 census in Summit, Alabama. Five more children had been born by then. Three of them had already died. The remaining two, Tetie and my grandfather, John, would be the only children of Richard and Mary Covington to live into the twentieth century.

Dad didn't know who the parents of Richard and Mary Covington were or where exactly they had lived in North Carolina or what had happened between 1860 and 1880, years during which they migrated from North Carolina to Alabama. Searching the microfilm at the Southern Collection of the Birmingham Public Library, I finally found the family at another location in Alabama in the 1870 census. Prior to the years in Summit, Richard and Mary Covington and their children had lived just south of Huntsville, at a place called Valhermosa Springs. The census taker had described both my great-grandfather and great-grandmother as illiterate. He had also checked the boxes for deaf, dumb, blind, insane, and idiotic. That was the end of what I knew about the Covingtons.

But Dad had been able to go back one generation further on his mother's side. My grandmother Covington had been a Howell. Her father had been born near Morristown, Tennessee, her mother in Nashville; at some point, they had migrated to that ridgetop called Summit, Alabama, where my grandmother, Hattie, was born. Hattie's mother's people had been Leas, and it was this line that my father had gotten the most information about. In particular, he had discovered that my great-great-grandfather, Benjamin Franklin Lea, also a Tennessean by birth, had served for three and a half years in the Confederate Army, and had been captured and held for six months in a Union prison camp. After the war, he became a Methodist circuit-riding preacher in northeastern Alabama. The center of his first circuit was Larkinsville, a town four miles west of Scottsboro.

Scottsboro. Glenn Summerford's home.

I felt as though I were closing in on the resolution of a mystery. I wondered what kind of doctrine my great-great-grandfather had been preaching in the precise area where snake handling would spring up less than a generation after his death. My reading in the history of American religion suggested an answer. John Wesley, the founder of Methodism, had challenged believers, through his doctrine of sanctification, to lead lives that were holy and set apart from sin. After the Civil War, with America's rapid urban industrialization and secularization, the calls for holiness became more strident and pervasive within American Methodism. The chief tenet of this Holiness movement was that after "salvation" or "new birth," there occurred a second act of grace, which believers called the "Baptism of the Holy Spirit." The result of this baptism, whether immediate or gradual, was moral purification. Later, the phrase also came to mean, for many believers, anyway, an imbuement of power from on high, as evidenced by spiritual gifts. Signs and wonders. Healing, prophecy, casting out devils, and ultimately speaking in tongues. My great-great-grandfather rode on horseback to preach baptism of the Holy Spirit to congregations around Scottsboro and most likely on top of Sand Mountain, where Methodist camp meetings, complete with brush arbors, drew enthusiastic crowds. *My great-great-grandfather had probably preached brush-arbor meetings on top of Sand Mountain.* I have no reason to believe he took up serpents, but I do have reason to believe he was a precursor of those who eventually did. In 1870, when he began his circuit-riding ministry in Alabama, Methodism was in the sway of the Holiness movement. It flourished for the next two decades, and broke out of Methodism only in the years immediately following his death, when the Methodist Church, its ranks swollen by middle-class urbanites, officially distanced itself from the rural and generally lower-class believers in sanctification and spiritual gifts. Out of Methodism came Holiness. Out

of Holiness came Pentecostalism. Out of the Holiness-
Pentecostal belief in spiritual signs and gifts came those who
took up serpents.

Carl Porter's father, for instance, had gotten the Holy
Ghost in a Methodist church in Alabama. Whether we were
blood related or not, the handlers and the Covingtons at
least shared the same spiritual ancestry. And about the time I
came to this realization, a librarian in the Southern Collection
of the Birmingham Public Library handed me a clip file containing, among other pieces, an Associated Press article from
1953, datelined Florence, Alabama:

SNAKE-HANDLING BROTHERS FINED $20 AND COSTS

FLORENCE, July 25 (AP) — Three snake handling brothers today
were fined $20 and costs for disturbing religious worship by
carrying a rattlesnake into a rural church.

Lauderdale County Law and Equity Court Judge Raymond
Murphy imposed the fines on Allen Covington, 37, and Mansel
and George Covington, 39.

The brothers had been held in the Lauderdale County Jail since
July 14, after they were arrested for a disturbance at the Bumpas
Creek Church.

Pat Murphy, one of the state witnesses, said that when the
brothers brought the snake into the church "The people sort of
scrounged back and acted like they were kind of afraid of it."

When asked by solicitor Frank Potts if the brothers broke up the service, Allen Covington replied, "The people broke it up themselves by leaving."

Mansel Covington, a big man dressed in overalls, held a Bible in his hands throughout the trial.

He said he and his brothers walked into the church and sat down in the "Amen corner." Mansel said they were praising the Lord.

George Covington testified that he had heard of an Alabama law against snake-handling and the brothers were expecting to be jailed.

"But we felt that we were obeying the spirit of the Lord," he asserted.

The brothers were tried under a disturbing the peace statute, not under Alabama's anti-snake handling law.

Snake-handling Covington brothers! But there was more. Two years later, Mansel Covington and his sister, Anna Marie Covington Yost, were bitten by rattlesnakes during a service in Savannah, Tennessee. Both were under suspended sentences for snake handling at the time. Mansel stubbornly refused treatment until the county coroner physically dragged him to a doctor for antivenin injections and then to jail. Anna Marie also refused treatment, and the next morning she died.

There were seven children in this family of Covington snake handlers, three daughters and four sons. All were born in Alabama. The sons are dead now. But Anna Marie's two sisters are still alive. Edna Covington, eighty, still lives in

Savannah, Tennessee. I tracked her down and visited with her in the living room of the modest brick home to which she had retired after thirty-one years as a registered nurse, most spent at the Veterans Administration Hospital in Louisville, Kentucky.

Edna was compact and athletic looking, with short-cropped sandy hair and a clipped accent. She invited me to join her on the floor, where she had been thumbing through a genealogy book in preparation for my visit. I didn't know whether Edna and I were related, but she looked like a member of our family. She had our sharp chin and deep-set eyes. Her Covingtons, she said, had settled on the north bank of the Tennessee River, at a place called Rogersville, Alabama. My great-grandfather and his family, on the other hand, had settled on the south bank of the Tennessee River, forty miles away, at Valhermosa Springs.

In 1932 Edna's family followed the natural curve of the Tennessee River up to Savannah, Tennessee, a stone's throw from Shiloh, where the seeds of the South's defeat had been sown, and the twentieth century conceived. That's where Edna's brothers and one of her sisters took up serpents. Edna never handled any.

"My brothers got into snake handling at outdoor camp meetings," she said. "They were just fooling around. They didn't keep busy enough."

Mansel Covington was the most outspoken of the brothers, she said. He was a big man in later life, but he had been born prematurely. "He was like a little rat," she said, continuing to flip through the pages of her book. "We'd put him on pillows to handle him. He couldn't talk till he was seven or eight." She paused to scan a list of names that may or may not have been her Covingtons. "Mansel and William were both eunuchs," she said matter-of-factly.

I asked what she meant.

Edna gave me a sharp look. "They had high voices and couldn't grow beards."

I wanted to hear more about this.

"They were born without testicles," she enunciated clearly, as though I were dense, and then lay her book aside.

As a young man, she said, Mansel worked in the freezer department at the Peabody Hotel in Memphis. He took hormone shots and began to shave, but he didn't like his job in the city, so he came back to Savannah and started going to outdoor revivals, where he eventually took up serpents. Edna's sister Anna Marie married and moved to Akron, Ohio, but she came back to Savannah alone and began going to snake-handling services with her brothers.

When Anna Marie got bit and died at the end of a two-week revival in 1956, Edna was working the night shift at the VA Hospital in Louisville. She didn't see any reason to rush back to Savannah, since Anna Marie was already dead, but her brother George, the one with the harelip, insisted that she leave work right then and drive all night to get back. George said he and his brothers were going to raise Anna Marie from the dead through prayer, and since Edna was a nurse, he wanted her to be there to check her sister's vital signs.

"There was a big full moon that night," Edna said.

I left Edna's house in Savannah, Tennessee, with that image in my head, of a woman driving all night under a full moon so that she could check her dead sister's vital signs while their brothers attempted to pray her back to life. I still didn't know whether Edna's family and mine were related. All I knew was that we had settled on opposite banks of the same river. Edna's band of Covingtons went one way, toward Shiloh, and wound up handling snakes. Our band kept coming south, first to Summit, and finally, in 1907, to Birmingham, where my father would be born and I would be born and my daughters would be born. Borderers. Hill people. New Lights.

When I told Carl Porter that I might have run across some handlers in my family tree, he seemed amused, but not surprised. "Who knows but that God sent you up here to write about Glenn's trial so you could find out that very thing?" he said.

Brother Carl had come from a family of Alabama share-croppers. He knew even less about his ancestors than I knew about mine. Unlike me, though, Carl seemed to have an intuitive grasp of the sort of people they were, and he had accepted it as the natural order of things. I was a city boy still trying to make sense of the notes in my father's green binder. My journey with the snake handlers had become not so much a linear progression through time as a falling through levels of platitude toward some hard understanding of who I was. I did not know where or when I would arrive at my destination. All I knew for certain was that snakes would be waiting for me there.

7
SNAKES

———

A few months after the New Year's Eve watch service, I was
in Atlanta on a magazine assignment, and I couldn't resist
the temptation to drive up to Kingston and visit with Brother
Carl. He'd recently bricked the outside of his double-wide
trailer across the highway from The Church of the Lord
Jesus Christ, and he seemed happy to see me.

By now, I believe Brother Carl thought of himself as a
spiritual mentor to me. In some ways, he was. He had taught
me about snake handling from the inside out. He'd also
encouraged me to read the entire New Testament straight
through, something I'd never done before. The previous summer, I had even considered asking him to baptize me in the
Tennessee River, but I finally decided to be baptized in my
home church in Birmingham instead. Getting baptized by a

snake-handling preacher is one thing; explaining it to family
and friends is another.

When we sat down at his kitchen table for coffee, he got
his Bible out and began steering me through some of his
favorite passages of scripture. He had on a blue dress shirt
and striped tie. On the kitchen counter lay his western-style
hat with the quail feathers stuck in the band. Carl loved to
feast on the Word. That's what he called it, feasting, as
though the Bible were a banquet set for him.

"The Bible says you're gonna suffer for your faith," he said
in his soft Georgia accent, which differed only in degree
from my own. "Look what happened to Stephen. I'd rather
die of snakebite than get stoned to death. And what about
Peter? Didn't they crucify him upside down on a cross? I'd
rather die of snakebite."

He glanced over the top of his glasses to gauge my reaction. It sounded like a toss-up to me.

Carl reminded me that he'd been bitten plenty of times by
poisonous snakes. The bites had hurt bad, and he didn't
want to get bit again. But he said he intended to keep on
doing the will of the Lord. He'd served four months in jail
back in the mid-1970s for disturbing public worship and for
aggravated assault with a deadly weapon — snakes. All he'd
done was take a few rattlesnakes into another man's church.
"We were invited," he said. A few years later, the lure of the

world proved too much for him. He left preaching for seven years. Carl spent much of those years on the road, driving big rigs to the West Coast and doing drugs and chasing women. His cousin, Gene Sherbert, kept the church going in his absence, while Carolyn waited for him to return to his senses and start taking up serpents again.

Now that he'd been back in the fold for almost seventeen years, Carl wasn't about to back up on the Lord. "I've been high on dope, whiskey," he said. "It's like nothing compared to the Spirit." He'd even handled cobras and coral snakes, he said. In my estimation, that was taking the idea of repentance too far.

At a quarter to seven, Carl said we'd better get on over to the church. When he got up from the table, he looked distracted and grave, like any other Southern preacher with a sermon on his mind. He thoughtfully put on his coat and picked up his Bible and looked around the place to see if he'd forgotten anything. The kitchen adjoined a large and comfortable living room with paneled walls, bookshelves filled with photos of his children and grandchildren, and a big TV and VCR. Nothing at all out of the ordinary.

Then Carl opened the door to the laundry room. Inside were three serpent boxes and two aquariums, containing a total of ten rattlesnakes, eight copperheads, and a cottonmouth moccasin. Carl opened the lid of a bright blue box with five timber rattlers in it. Three of them stuck their heads out. "Get on back in there," he said as he tapped each of them gently on the nose with his finger.

It had been almost a year since I'd covered Glenn Summerford's trial, and I'd gotten to know the handlers well enough by then not to be too surprised when Carl tapped those rattlesnakes on the head. It was kind of a sweet gesture, I thought. I helped him load the snakes into the trunk of his car.

Outside, it was a clear, cold night.

"On New Year's Eve, you looked like you wanted to handle one," he said.

I didn't answer. That particular feeling had passed. But I was open to mystery in a way I had never been in mainstream churches. It was not beyond the realm of possibility that I would one day get the urge again to take up a serpent.

Carl smiled at me and slammed the trunk lid shut. "It's like nothing that's ever happened to you," he said. "You'll *know* then why we do it."

What I didn't tell Carl that night was that I had handled snakes all my life, but not, of course, in church. When I was a boy, I'd catch common water snakes in Village Creek, an open sewer that ran through the heart of Birmingham. These snakes weren't poisonous, but they had nasty temperaments. And they were exceptionally ugly. Their banded markings disappeared with age. The older ones had dull, olive skin with keeled scales, and when they were excited, they emitted a bad-smelling fluid from scent glands at the base of their tails. Only their numbers recommended them. Village Creek teemed with these water snakes, and they were not that difficult to catch. I'd set out minnow traps in deep water under the Eightieth Street bridge. When I'd caught enough minnows to use as bait, I'd reset the traps in shallow water farther downstream, under the twisted willows or Tupelo black gum that grew along the banks. When the creek flooded during summer thunderstorms, these bushes would catch the city's refuse — soggy wads of newsprint and toilet paper, rubbers, used Kotex, wigs and nylon hose, children's stuffed animals, shoes, men's plastic raincoats, and, occasionally, a woman's brassiere.

The best time to set the traps for common water snakes was a few days after the rains had ended. By then, the water would have cleared. Sometimes I'd catch two or three snakes in a single trap. These were generally medium-sized snakes, ones that could fit through the opening in the inverted cone-shaped end of the trap. The biggest water snakes, the four or five footers, basked in the hot sun on higher ground. My friend Beaver Morrison and I would hunt them with sticks and a shovel in the cauliflower field that fronted the creek. The field was owned by Italians. They lived in turquoise houses at the end of the alley, and pretty much kept to themselves. Most of the time, we'd forget the Italians even lived there, until it rained and the whole neighborhood smelled of cauliflower.

When approached in the open, these big water snakes would head for old rodent burrows deep in the weeds, and most of the time they would make it there before we could catch them. Sometimes, though, Beaver or I would get hold of a big, nasty water snake before it could completely disappear down the hole. I remember the thick, dry bodies, the uncanny strength. One of us would hold on to the snake. The other guy would use the shovel to dig out the burrow, and the freed snake, a blur of ocher and olive, would turn, charge out of the collapsing dirt like a bull. I've been bitten by common water snakes. It's nothing, a humiliation more than a pain. But I know how snakes work, the physics of the bite. It's not something to take lightly, even among nonpoisonous snakes. You can never predict what a snake will do.

At certain times of the year in Birmingham, we could find baby water snakes under the rocks on the sandbar beneath the Eightieth Street bridge. They were bright and exquisitely detailed, with coppery, saddle-shaped bands and yellow jawlines, but they were also very quick. You couldn't stop to wonder whether they were baby copperheads or not. You had to grab fast, without really looking, or they'd be gone. If you caught one, though, you were just as well to let it go. Baby water snakes didn't do well in captivity. An adult, at least, though ugly, might occasionally eat a frog.

There were plenty of frogs, and turtles, too, at East Lake, a short walk down the alley from my house. Unlike the names of residential neighborhoods these days, ours referred to a real thing, a lake three blocks long and one block wide. There had been an amusement park there in my father's day, with a roller coaster, a tunnel of love, and pedal-driven boats. All that was left by the time my childhood rolled around were man-made jetties and a rock balustrade. I'd go to the lake just about every day after school to hunt for turtles, but I was also on the lookout for snakes. Village Creek paralleled the lake, with more water snakes, but of a different kind. We called them queen snakes, and I thought for many years that we had invented the name, until I found it in a snake book and knew from the photos that they were ours. Unlike the common water snakes, the queen snakes had no visible pattern on their backs at all. They were a smooth and even brown, a light caramel. But underneath, along the edges of their bellies, ran two sets of paired stripes, one gold, one green, like ribbons, iridescent in the sun. The queen snakes were agile climbers. They could not be caught in minnow traps or on the ground with sticks and shovels. They always sunned in the leafy branches of the willows and Tupelo bushes along the banks. A snake noose attached to a broom handle was the only way to catch them. And even then, they were hard to snare. The rawhide noose had to be slipped over their heads without touching, and deftly pulled tight.

The approach was the key. Slow and incremental, without vibrating a single leaf. Queen snakes could drop into the water in the intake of a breath. Hunting them, I learned to be patient. I also learned to accept the inevitability of occasional defeat.

On Saturdays, for variety, Beaver and I would hike to the city dump by the airport, the best place to find long, elegant green snakes and the tiny brown snakes called Dekay's snakes, after the guy who first classified them. Dekay's snakes could also be found in the flower beds of East Lake yards. When neighbors told stories about ground rattlers in the begonias, these were the snakes they most often were talking about. And then there were always ring-necked snakes and worm snakes, but these were so small and secretive, they most often went unnoticed by gardeners my parents' age. The best snakes, the absolutely best snakes of all, came from Ruffner Mountain, a foothill of the Appalachians that overlooked East Lake. It was just out of walking distance from my house. We only tried walking it once. Other times, my father drove and dropped us off. We said we were hiking to the fire tower at the top of the mountain. But I always had my eyes peeled for snakes.

The first snake I caught on Ruffner Mountain was a corn snake I saw wrapped around the trunk of a pine tree. Docile and graceful, it had scarlet blotches and an intricately patterned head, as surprising as though it were a piece of Arabian carpet found dangling in the Alabama woods. The corn snake ate mice, but I couldn't bear to keep it long, even though my father had made me a first-rate snake cage with the power tools he'd bought after someone told him he needed a hobby. I let that corn snake go one day in the Italians' cauliflower field and always hoped that I would see it again. I never did.

My friend Bert Butts gave me my second Ruffner Mountain snake. It was a speckled king, big and black, freshly shed, with tiny yellow splotches from head to tail, as though a paintbrush had been shaken lightly over it. King snakes are famous for their placid dispositions. Like marine mammals, they seem to wear a perpetual smile, and they happen to eat rattlesnakes. I named this king snake Kuebert Wood, after a track star at a local high school. He would sunbathe on my stomach. I swore I'd never let him go. But then I caught a gigantic gray rat snake, five and a half feet, a record, I thought. I gave the rat snake the cage my father had built and relegated Kuebert Wood to a number-ten washtub with a screen on top, held down by rocks. During the night, Kuebert escaped. Well, I prefer to think he wandered off. I have hated the memory of that rat snake ever since.

A final gift came from a friend named Galen Bailey, who lived closer to the mountain than I did. This snake was very delicate and rare, a scarlet snake, with alternate rings of red, black, and yellow. Except for the broken rings and the order of the colors, it looked exactly like a coral snake: quite perfect, but it wouldn't eat. I kept it longer than I should have, because of its beauty. I hope it survived after I released it in the cauliflower field. With snakes, you never know.

The poisonous snakes came later, when I was an adult. I have caught only three, and I did not keep any of them overnight. The first was a pygmy rattlesnake I found sunning on a grave in a cemetery in southwestern Louisiana, where I was stationed while in the army in the early 1970s. The pygmy rattlesnake is a small, stout snake, rarely over two feet in length. It is ill-tempered and can deliver a painful bite. Its venom is as powerful as that of larger rattlesnakes, but since less venom is injected at a time, the bites of pygmy rattlers are rarely life-threatening.

This particular snake looked plenty dangerous to me, though. I was hung over. My first wife and I had taken a Sunday drive to visit old cemeteries. It was spring. Tarantulas were crossing the road in droves. When I saw the pygmy rattlesnake on the grave, it seemed to be a sign. I had to conquer my fear of it. My heart beat faster. My palms ached. I found a stick, pinned the snake behind the head, and picked it up. My wife was horrified when I told her what it was. She'd hunted nonpoisonous snakes with me, but this was a little much.

The problem, I discovered, was not in catching the snake, but in releasing it. How do you let a rattlesnake go without risking a bite? I wound up taking the steps in nearly reverse order: putting it on the ground, pinning it with the stick, and only then releasing my grip. It worked. I had accomplished something. The marriage lasted another four years.

The second poisonous snake was a copperhead I found stretched out on a road on Red Mountain in Birmingham, the last snake of the summer. I was married to Vicki by then and teaching at the university. Again, I was hung over. I brought the snake home, stretched between my hands, and told Vicki to find an empty ice chest to put it in. She, too, was horrified. Then we drove into the country to let it go. I wrote a short story about the way it looked coming out of the ice chest and disappearing into the dark woods.

Then I sobered up. We had our girls and built a house in the woods on the side of Sand Mountain. The last poisonous snake I caught was a canebrake rattlesnake that was crossing the pavement at the bottom of our driveway. I brought it up to the house so the girls could get a good look and know what kind of snake to avoid. Then I said I was going to let it go in the woods. I killed it instead. I do not believe it is necessary for a man to allow a poisonous snake to cross his property while his children are young. It is the only snake I have ever killed like that. It still bothers me some.

There are two families of poisonous snakes in the United States, both of them native to our part of the South. The first, *Elapidae,* which include cobras, mambas, and other deadly Old World snakes, are represented in the New World by eastern and western coral snakes. Coral snakes are shy, beautiful, and extremely dangerous. Their venom is a neurotoxin that attacks the central nervous system, particularly autonomic functions such as breathing and heartbeat. Fortunately, coral snakes are reclusive by nature. They seldom bite, and when they do, their small mouths and fixed fangs make it difficult for them to successfully latch on to humans.

The second family of poisonous snakes, the *Crotalidae,* contain the pit vipers — rattlesnakes, copperheads, and cottonmouths. The pits for which these snakes are named are infrared-heat-sensing organs that lie between the nostrils and eyes. With them, the snakes hunt their warm-blooded prey by seeking out body heat. The pit vipers are efficient killers, with large, flexible mouths; long, retractable fangs; and venom that attacks and destroys cells and tissue. Victims die of internal hemorrhaging, cardiovascular shock, or kidney and respiratory failure.

The least dangerous of the pit vipers to man is the copper-head, although its bite can, and does, kill children. The most dangerous is the eastern diamondback rattlesnake, which can grow to a length of eight feet and has a combative temperament and a large reservoir of venom. Somewhere in between lies the timber rattler, often called the canebrake rattlesnake in our part of the country. Herpetologists disagree about whether the canebrake is a color variation or a distinct subspecies. The timber rattler is the snake seen most often in serpent-handling churches, because it is the poisonous snake most readily available on the rocky hillsides and grassy valleys of the Appalachians. It shares its range with the copper-head, but appears to be more sociable, often found in large numbers in dens or burrows. The timber is somewhat smaller and less aggressive than the diamondback, but it is still a dangerous snake, unpredictable and with venom that can easily kill an adult.

The timber rattler is also, to me, the loveliest of the rattlesnakes, varying in color from pink to straw to nearly uniform black, with sharp, dark chevrons on its back. Its neck is narrow and girlish, its head as finely defined as an arrow. Oftentimes the body of the snake is velvety in appearance. In such cases, the handlers will call the snake a "satinback." Encountered in the wild, a large timber rattler, *Crotalus horridus*, is an impressive and frightening sight. When cornered, it rattles energetically and coils to strike. But its first impulse is to flee, and perhaps that, too, is a source of its beauty: a dangerous animal, exquisitely made, turning away from a fight.

In captivity, timber rattlers can live up to thirty years. Their tenure among the handlers is much shorter, rarely exceeding a season. I have seen timber rattlers die while being handled. They are not made to be jerked around like that. On the other hand, some of the snakes are well cared for, but simply released into the wild after a few months. Handlers don't like to keep snakes that look puny, and they are always in search of new ones, always trading specimens back and forth. It appears to be a ritual after services for handlers to give snakes to one another, like an offering of brandy or after-dinner mints or hand-rolled cigars in other circles. Some of the handlers regularly catch their own snakes, most of the time in conventional ways, with a snake stick and burlap bag or pillowcase. Occasionally, the Holiness hunters will fall under an anointing to handle right there in the woods. Others buy snakes from professional exhibitors at prices the handlers complain are getting more outrageous every year, as much as forty-five dollars at last reckoning.

However the snakes are obtained, they often become objects of affection in the homes of the handlers and their families. The first rattlesnake that Aline McGlocklin took up, for instance, was called Old Crooked Neck, because of the injury it had received during capture. The big copperhead in the terrarium on the McGlocklins' kitchen counter used to be called Mr. Hog, Charles said, until it had eight babies and they had to start calling it Miss Piggy instead. And Darlene Summerford had testified at Glenn's trial that the photographs she carried in her purse were of her favorite rattlesnake.

But no amount of affection or care can insure that a rattlesnake or copperhead won't bite when handled. They do not tame in a conventional sense. They are not hamsters or gerbils. No one can predict what will happen when a handler reaches into the serpent box. And contrary to popular misconception, multiple bites do not result in immunity to snake venom, but may even increase the risk of death because of allergic reaction.

Around eight thousand people in the United States are bitten each year by poisonous snakes. Of this number, only a dozen or so die. Experts advise that the best first aid is to keep the patient calm and get him to a hospital as quickly as possible. Based on the severity of the bite, doctors determine whether to use antivenin therapy. Sometimes the risk of an adverse reaction from the antivenin is of as much concern as the bite itself. Recent literature suggests electric shocks administered to the site of the bite may be helpful, but research about this therapy has been inconclusive.

To date, at least seventy-one people have been killed by poisonous snakes during religious services in the United

States, including the man said to have started the whole thing, George Went Hensley, who died vomiting blood in a shed in North Florida in 1955. Hensley had started handling around 1910 and had been bitten more than four hundred times before the fatal blow. Scholars attribute to him the spread of snake handling beyond Grasshopper Valley to other parts of Tennessee, and to Kentucky, the Carolinas, Virginia, Ohio, and Indiana.

But snake handling sprang up independently on Sand Mountain around 1912, the work of a former Baptist preacher named James Miller. As early as 1934, poisonous snakes were being taken up in outdoor worship services in the eastern part of Birmingham, among racially mixed congregations. The only recorded injury from these early days was sustained by a man named N.C. Brownlee, who fell off a roof while trying to get a better look at a rattlesnake brought to a service in a glass bread case. The rattlesnake's name was Pete.

"The first place that I ever heard of people handling serpents," Charles McGlocklin once told me, "was just the other side of New Hope, Alabama, when I was seven or eight years old." That would have been in the late 1940s. "In those days," Charles said, "they kept the serpents in lard cans in the smokehouse."

The Alabama legislature apparently got wind of the practice and passed an act in 1950 that made it "unlawful for any person to display, handle, exhibit or use any poisonous or dangerous snake or reptile in such a manner as to endanger the life or health of another." The crime was described as a felony, with a prescribed punishment of one to five years imprisonment. But the handling continued in spite of the law.

In 1951, a New Hope farm wife named Ruthie Craig, fifty, brought a glass jar containing a large rattlesnake into religious services at her home. "I'm going to handle the snake and anyone who doesn't believe had better leave," she said. Then she tried to extract the snake from the jar. It wouldn't budge, so she broke the glass. The rattlesnake slithered onto the floor and toward an open door. Mrs. Craig tried to catch it, but it turned on her and bit her four times on the right forearm and shoulder before it escaped. Asked later if she wanted a doctor, Mrs. Craig said, "Anything for ease." But someone in the congregation said she would lose her faith if she called a doctor, so Mrs. Craig rejected help, fell into a coma, and died four hours later. The Madison County coroner ruled it an accident.

The death of Ruthie Craig was the first in a string of highly publicized fatalities among handlers in North Alabama and Georgia during the 1950s. Sawmill worker Jim Thomas Gifford died in Fort Payne, Alabama, in 1954; lay preacher Reece Ramsey died two months later at a brush-arbor meet-

ing south of Rising Fawn, Georgia; and Lee Valentine, a
father of seven, was bitten at the Old Straight Creek Holiness
Church on top of Sand Mountain in August of 1955. He
died a few hours later. All had refused medical help.

In 1956, Lloyd Hill of Fort Payne, the first man tried and
convicted under the Alabama snake-handling law, came to
Birmingham and was bitten on the hand by a rattlesnake at a
church on the outskirts of East Lake, at the foot of Ruffner
Mountain. He was taken to the old Hillman Clinic emergency
room, where he refused treatment. Charged for a second
time with snake handling, he discovered his next stop was
the city jail and then the county jail, where he made his three-
hundred-dollar bond and promptly disappeared.

Lloyd Hill survived that bite. Another preacher who handled snakes in Birmingham didn't. David Henson, a retired
coal shaker operator who had been preaching and handling
for thirty years, died in 1959 less than an hour after being
bitten by a twenty-four-pound rattlesnake in Robinwood, a
working-class neighborhood just the other side of the
Birmingham airport from East Lake. Henson's death was
ruled a suicide, although members of the congregation at his
Free Holiness Church knew otherwise. Close to a thousand
people filed by his open coffin to pay respects. On our side
of the airport, in that same year, a black man was kidnapped
and later castrated by members of the Ku Klux Klan. I can-

not help but believe there is a connection between the two events. Henson's funeral was conducted at Roebuck Chapel, where my father's funeral would be held thirty years later. My father was not a snake handler, but he was a segregationist.

There are snakes, and there are snakes. Some are literal, some not. While I was handling common water snakes in a sewer at the end of our street in East Lake, people were taking up rattlesnakes in a church a few blocks away. We didn't know them. They didn't know us. We might as well have occupied parallel universes, except for one thing: we had come from the same place. We were border dwellers. We had sailed for the promised land. We had entered the mountains and come down from them again. We were the same people. And all of us were handling one kind of snake or another.

The literal snakes are the easiest to identify: my water snakes, their rattlesnakes. The metaphorical snakes are another matter. One of them, I see now, must have been our uncertain past. When I was growing up in East Lake, among families reaching for the middle class, the past was problematic and embarrassing because it contained poverty, ignorance, racism, and defeat. This legacy of Southern history was as dangerous as any rattlesnake. No one wanted to claim it. No one wanted to take it out of the box. No one, of course, except the Klansmen who paraded past our house on

Eightieth Street in the 1950s, their lead car bearing a cross made of light bulbs. How strange those processions at twilight seem to me now, how out of place on the quiet streets of East Lake. I wonder why my father didn't sound the alarm. During World War II, he had been a civil defense warden for our neighborhood. My older brothers said that during air raid drills, he would stand on the darkened street corner in his white pith helmet with the civil defense insignia on the front and smoke a cigarette as he looked for low-flying enemy planes. Where was he when the Klan motorcades came down Eightieth Street?

Dad had no use for the Klan. He was a gentle, principled man. But he must have sensed even then that the past he seemed bent on avoiding was bound to be claimed by someone, somewhere along the line. He was, as I've said, in theory if not in practice, a segregationist. Some of his arguments seem tamer now in retrospect, tempered as they are by time. But he was still a segregationist, in an era when legal segregation was our greatest shame. The bombing of the Sixteenth Street Baptist Church in Birmingham in 1963 broke my father's resistance, and his heart. The girls who died in the bombing were about my age. We heard the news on a small brown radio in the kitchen after church that Sunday. It was the first time I ever saw my father cry. The bombing seemed to seal a permanent judgment on the city. "The shame will be ours forever," editorialized a local newspaper at the time. But Martin Luther King, Jr., foresaw ultimate salvation in the tragedy. At the funeral for three of the girls, he said, "The deaths may well serve as the redemptive force that brings light to this dark city." And it did. What happened in Birmingham in 1963 not only redeemed the oppressed. It also redeemed my people, although we haven't been able to accept that yet. We haven't yet taken that particular snake out and lifted it aloft in the light — the dangerous, unloved thing about us: where we came from, what we did, who we are.

I don't know exactly when it happened, but sometime during the spring of 1993, the idea must have started taking shape that in order to conquer the metaphorical snake that was my cultural legacy, I'd have to take up the thing itself.

8

SALVATION ON
SAND MOUNTAIN

---

*And a vision appeared to Paul in the night; There stood
a man of Macedonia, and prayed him, saying, Come
over into Macedonia, and help us.*

— Acts 16:9

That spring, Charles McGlocklin told me that Glenn
Summerford's cousins, Billy and Jimmy, had started a new
church on top of Sand Mountain, near a place called
Macedonia. Charles didn't worship with them, though.

"Why not?" I asked.

Brother Charles took a deep breath and surveyed the land
around him, yellow and gray in the afternoon light. We were
on the deck behind his and Aline's trailer in New Hope,
Alabama. Beside the trailer was a doghouse for their blue
tick hound named Smokey, and behind it was a corral for
their horse, a buckskin mare named Dixie Honeydew.

"I know enough about some of those people to know I
ought not to worship anymore with them," Charles said. As
a snake handler, he had set himself apart from the world,
and sometimes he even set himself apart from other snake

handlers. It was part of the Southern character, I thought, to be always turning away like that toward some secret part of oneself.

"You know how much I love you," Charles said. He put one of his big hands on my shoulder and shook it. "You're my brother. But anytime you go up there on Sand Mountain, you be careful."

We could hear the sound of the wind through trees, a soughing, dry and hesitant, and then Dixie Honeydew neighed.

"You might be anointed when you take up a serpent," Charles continued, "but if there's a witchcraft spirit in the church, it could zap your anointing and you'd be left cold turkey with a serpent in your hand and the spirit of God gone off of you. That's when you'll get bit."

We walked around the corner of the trailer, where Jim Neel was waiting for me in a truck that had belonged to his brother.

"So you really watch and remember what Brother Charles tells you," Charles whispered. "Always be careful who you take a rattlesnake from."

This sounded like solid advice.

I got into Jim's truck, and Charles motioned for us to roll a window down. "Y'all come back any time," he yelled. "And, hey, it's not us that's messed up, Brother Dennis. It's the world."

. . .

My journey had come back around to the congregation on Sand Mountain, the remnant of Glenn Summerford's flock that had left the converted service station on Wood's Cove Road in Scottsboro and then met under a brush arbor in back of J.L. Dyal's house until the weather got too cold. After worshiping for a while in the basement of an old motel, they finally found a church for sale on the mountain. It was miles from nowhere, in the middle of a hay field south of Section, Alabama, home of Tammy Little, Miss Alabama 1984. The nearest dot on the map, though, was Macedonia, a crossroads consisting of a filling station, a country store, and a junk emporium. It was not the kind of place you'd visit of your own accord. You'd have to be led there. In fact, Macedonia had gotten its name from the place in the Bible that Paul had been called to go to in a dream. Paul's first European converts to Christianity had been in Macedonia. But that was, you know, a long time ago and in another place.

Glenn Summerford's cousins, Billy and Jimmy, negotiated the deal for the church. Billy was friendly and loose limbed, with a narrow red face and buck teeth. He'd worked mostly as a carpenter, but he'd also sold coon dogs. Jimmy was less amiable but more compact. Between them, they must have been persuasive. They got the church for two thousand dollars. A guy down the road had offered five thousand, Billy said, but the owner had decided to sell it to them. "God was working in that one," he concluded.

It was called the Old Rock House Holiness Church, in spite of the fact that it wasn't made of rock. But it was old in contrast to the brick veneer churches out on highway 35, the ones with green indoor-outdoor carpet in the vestibules and blinking U-Haul It signs out front.

The Old Rock House Holiness Church had been built in 1916, a few years before Dozier Edmonds first saw people take up serpents in Jackson County, at a church in Sauty Bottom, down by Saltpeter Cave. I'd met Dozier during the brush-arbor meetings. A rail-thin old man with thick glasses and overalls, he was the father-in-law of J.L. Dyal and the husband of Burma, the snake-handling twin. Dozier said he'd seen men get bit in that church in Sauty Bottom. They didn't go to a doctor, just swelled up a little bit. He also remembered a Holiness boy at the one-room school who would fall into a trance, reach into the potbellied stove, and get himself a whole handful of hot coals. The teacher would have to tell the boy to put them back. There was a Baptist church in those days called Hell's Half Acre, Dozier said. They didn't take up serpents, but they'd do just about anything else. They were called Buckeye Baptists. They'd preach and pray till midnight, then gamble and fight till dawn. One time a man rode a horse into the church, right up to the pul-

pit. Out of meanness, Dozier said. Everything was different
then. "They used to tie the mules up to a white mulberry
bush in the square," he said. Why, he remembered when
Scottsboro itself was nothing but a mud hole. When the car-
nival came through, the elephants were up to their bellies in
mud. There wasn't even a road up Sand Mountain until
Dozier helped build one. And it seemed like the Civil War
had just occurred.

Dozier came from a family of sharecroppers who lived on
the property of a famous Confederate veteran named Mance.
He had a bullet hole through his neck. He'd built his own casket. Every Easter, Colonel Mance invited the children of the
families who lived on his property to come to the big house
for an egg hunt. One Easter, he wanted the children to see
what he'd look like when he was dead, so he lay down in the
casket and made the children march around it. Some of the
grown-ups had to help get him out. It was a pine casket with
metal handles on it, Dozier said. Colonel Mance eventually
died, but he wasn't buried in the casket he'd made. He'd
taken that thing apart years before and given the handles to
the families who lived on his property, to use as knockers on
the doors of their shacks.

That was the kind of place Sand Mountain had been when
the Old Rock House Holiness Church was in its heyday. By
the time the Summerford brothers bought it in the winter of
1993, it had fallen onto hard times. Didn't even have a back

door. Paper wasps had built nests in the eaves. The green shingles on the outside were cracked, and the paint on the window sills had just about peeled off. Billy Summerford and some of the other men from the congregation repaired and restored the church as best they could. It'd be another year, though, before they could get around to putting in a bathroom. In the meantime, there would be an outhouse for the women and a bunch of trees for the men. The church happened to be sited in the very center of a grove of old oak trees. Fields of hay surrounded the grove and stretched to the horizon. As you approached the church along a dirt road during summer heat, the oak grove looked like a dark island in the middle of a shimmering sea of gold and green.

That's the way it looked to me, anyway, on a bright Sunday morning in late June, six months after the Summerfords had bought the church, when Jim and I drove up from Birmingham for their first annual homecoming. Brother Carl had invited us by phone and given us directions. He was scheduled to preach at the homecoming. Other handlers were coming from all over — from East Tennessee and South Georgia, from the mountains of Kentucky and the scrublands of the Florida panhandle. If we hadn't had Carl's directions, we'd never have found the place. The right turn off the paved road from Macedonia was unmarked. It was one of several gravel roads that angled off into the distance. Where it crossed another paved road, there finally was a sign, made of cardboard and mounted at waist level on a wooden stake. After that, the gravel turned to dirt. Dust coated the jimson-weed. The passionflowers were in bloom, and the blackber-ries had begun to ripen in the heat. There were no houses on this road, and no sound except for cicadas, a steady din, like the sound of approaching rain.

For once, Jim and I were early. We stepped up on a cement block to get through the back doorway of the church. The door itself was off its hinges, and none of the windows in the church had screens. There were no cushions on the pews and no ornaments of any kind, except a portrait of Jesus etched into a mirror behind the pulpit and a vase of plastic flowers on the edge of the piano bench, where a boy with a withered hand sat staring at the keys. We took our places on a back pew and watched the handlers arrive. They greeted each other with the holy kiss, women with women, men with men, as prescribed by Paul in Romans 16. Among them was the leg-endary Punkin Brown, the evangelist who I'd been told would wipe the sweat off his brow with rattlesnakes. Jamie Coots from Kentucky and Allen Williams from Tennessee were also there. They sat beside Punkin on the deacons' bench. All three were young and heavyset, the sons of preachers, and childhood friends. Punkin and Jamie both wore scowls, as though they were waiting for somebody to cross their paths in an unhappy way. Allen Williams, though, looked serene.

Allen's father had died drinking strychnine in 1973, and his brother had died of snakebite in 1991. Maybe he thought he didn't have anything more to lose. Or maybe he was just reconciled to losing everything he had. Within six months of sitting together on the deacons' bench at the Old Rock House Church, Jamie, Allen, and Punkin would all be bit.

The church continued to fill with familiar faces, many from what used to be The Church of Jesus with Signs Following in Scottsboro, and the music began without an introduction of any kind. James Hatfield of Old Straight Creek, a Trinitarian church on the mountain, was on drums. My red-haired friend Cecil Esslinder from Scottsboro was on guitar, grinning and tapping his feet. Cecil's wife, Carolyn, stood in the very middle of the congregation, facing backward, as was her habit, to see who might come in the back way. Also in the congregation were Bobbie Sue Thompson, twins Burma and Erma, J.L. Dyal and his wife and in-laws, and just about the whole Summerford clan. The only ones missing were Charles and Aline McGlocklin. Charles was still recovering from neck surgery on an old injury, but I knew from the conversation we'd had in New Hope that even if he'd been well, he wouldn't have come.

One woman I didn't recognize told me she was from Detroit, Michigan. This came as some surprise, and her story seemed equally improbable. She said her husband used to

work in the casinos in Las Vegas, and when he died she
moved to Alabama and started handling rattlesnakes at the
same church on Lookout Mountain where the lead singer of
the group Alabama used to handle. "Didn't you see the
photo?" she asked. "It was in the *National Enquirer*."

I told her I'd missed that one.

Children were racing down the aisles. High foreheads. Eyes
far apart. Gaps between their front teeth. They all looked
like miniature Glenn Summerfords. Maybe they were. He
had at least seven children by his first wife, and all of them
were old enough to have children of their own. I started to
wonder if there were any bad feelings among the Summerfords about the way Brother Carl Porter had refused to let
them send the church offerings to Glenn in prison.

About that time, Brother Carl himself walked in with a serpent box containing the biggest rattlesnake I'd ever seen.
Carl smelled of Old Spice and rattlesnake and something else
underneath: a pleasant smell, like warm bread and apples. I
associated it with the Holy Ghost. The handlers had told me
that the Holy Ghost had a smell, a "sweet savor," and I had
begun to think I could detect it on people and in churches,
even in staid, respectable churches like the one I went to in
Birmingham. Anyway, that was what I smelled on Brother
Carl that day as he talked about the snake in the box. "I just
got him today," he said. "He's never been in church before."
Carl looked over his glasses at me and smiled. He held the

serpent box up to my face and tapped the screen until the snake started rattling good.

"Got your name on him," he said to me.

A shiver went up my spine, but I just shook my head and grinned.

"Come on up to the front," he said. I followed him and sat on the first pew next to J.L. Dyal, but I made a mental note to avoid Carl's eyes during the service and to stay away from that snake of his.

Billy Summerford's wife, Joyce, led the singing. She was a big woman with a voice that wouldn't quit. *"Remember how it felt, when you walked out of the wilderness, walked out of the wilderness, walked out of the wilderness. Remember how it felt, when you walked out of the wilderness . . ."* It was one of my favorite songs because it had a double meaning now. There was the actual wilderness in the Old Testament that the Israelites were led out of, and the spiritual wilderness that was its referent, the condition of being lost. But there was also the wilderness that the New World became for my father's people. I don't mean the mountains. I mean the America that grew up around them, that tangled thicket of the heart.

"Remember how it felt, when you walked out of the wilderness . . ." My throat tightened as I sang. I remembered how it had felt when I'd sobered up in 1983. It's not often you get a second chance at life like that. And I remembered

the births of my girls, the children Vicki and I had thought we'd never be able to have. Looking around at the familiar faces in the congregation, I figured they were thinking about their own wildernesses and how they'd been delivered out of them. I was still coming out of mine. It was a measure of how far I'd come, that I'd be moved nearly to tears in a run-down Holiness church on Sand Mountain. But my restless and stubborn intellect was still intact. It didn't like what it saw, a crowd of men dancing up to the serpent boxes, unclasping the lids, and taking out the poisonous snakes. Reason told me it was too early in the service. The snakes hadn't been prayed over enough. There hadn't even been any preaching yet, just Billy Summerford screaming into a micro-phone while the music swirled around us like a fog. But the boys from Tennessee and Kentucky had been hungry to get into the boxes. Soon, Punkin Brown was shouting at his snake, a big black-phase timber rattler that he had draped around his neck. Allen Williams was offering his copperhead up like a sacrifice, hands outstretched. But Brother Carl had the prize, and everyone seemed to know it. It was a yellow-phase timber, thick and melancholy, as big as timber rattlers come. Carl glanced at me, but I wouldn't make eye contact with him. I turned away. I walked to the back of the church and took a long drink of water from the bright yellow cooler propped up against a portrait of Jesus with his head on fire.

"Who knows what this snake is thinking?" Carl shouted. "God knows! God understands the mind of this snake!" And when I turned back around, Carl had laid the snake down and was treading barefoot on it from tail to head, as though he were walking a tightrope. Still, the snake didn't bite. I had heard about this, but never seen it before. The passage was from Luke: *Behold, I give unto you power to tread on serpents and scorpions, and over all the power of the enemy: and nothing shall by any means hurt you.* Then Carl picked the snake back up and draped it around his neck. The snake seemed to be looking for a way out of its predicament. Carl let it nuzzle into his shirt. Then the snake pulled back and cocked its head, as if in preparation to strike Carl's chest. Its head was as big as a child's hand.

Help him, Jesus! someone yelled above the din. Instead of striking, the snake started to climb Carl's sternum toward his collarbone. It went up the side of his neck and then lost interest and fell back against his chest.

The congregation was divided into two camps now, the men to the left, with the snakes, the women to the right, with each other. In front of Carl, one of the men suddenly began jumping straight up and down, as though he were on a pogo stick. Down the aisle he went and around the sanctuary. When he returned, he collapsed at Carl's feet. One of the Summerford brothers attended to him there by soaking his handkerchief with olive oil and dabbing it against the man's forehead until he sat up and yelled, "Thank God!"

In the meantime, in the corner where the women had gathered, Joyce Summerford's sister, Donna, an attractive young woman in a lime green dress, was laboring in the spirit with a cataleptic friend. She circled the friend, eyeing her contortions carefully, and then, as if fitting her into an imaginary dress, she clothed her in the spirit with her hands, an invisible tuck here, an invisible pin there, making sure the spirit draped well over the flailing arms. It took her a while. Both of the women were drenched in sweat and stuttering in tongues by the time they finished.

"They say we've gone crazy!" Brother Carl shouted above the chaos. He was pacing in front of the pulpit, the enormous rattlesnake balanced now across his shoulder. "Well, they're right!" he cried. "I've gone crazy! I've gone Bible crazy! I've got the papers here to prove it!" And he waved his worn Bible in the air. "Some people say we're just a bunch of fanatics!"

Amen. Thank God.

"Well, we are! *Hai-i-salemos-ah-cahn-ne-hi-yee!* Whew! That last one nearly took me out of here!"

It's not true that you become used to the noise and confusion of a snake-handling Holiness service. On the contrary, you become enmeshed in it. It is theater at its most intricate

— improvisational, spiritual jazz. The more you experience it, the more attentive you are to the shifts in the surface and the dark shoals underneath. For every outward sign, there is a spiritual equivalent. When somebody falls to his knees, a specific problem presents itself, and the others know exactly what to do, whether it's oil for a healing, or a prayer cloth thrown over the shoulders, or a devil that needs to be cast out. The best, of course, the simplest and cleanest, is when someone gets the Holy Ghost for the first time. The younger the worshiper, the easier it seems to be for the Holy Ghost to descend and speak — lips loosened, tongue flapping, eyes rolling backward in the head. It transcends the erotic when a thirteen-year-old girl gets the Holy Ghost. The older ones often take time. I once saw an old man whose wife had gotten the Holy Ghost at a previous service. He wanted it bad for himself, he said. Brother Charles McGlocklin started praying with him before the service even started, and all through it, the man was in one attitude or another at the front of the church — now lying spread-eagled on the floor, while a half dozen men prayed over him and laid on hands, now up and running from one end of the sanctuary to the other, now twirling, now swooning, now collapsing once again on the floor, his eyes like the eyes of a horse that smells smoke, the unknown tongue spewing from his mouth. He got the Holy Ghost at last! He got the Holy Ghost! you think, until you see him after the service eating a pimiento cheese sandwich downstairs. His legs are crossed. He's brushing the crumbs from his lap. He agrees it was a good service all right, but it sure would have been better if he'd only gotten the Holy Ghost. You can never get enough of the Holy Ghost. Maybe that's what he means. You can never exhaust the power when the Spirit comes down, not even when you take up a snake, not even when you take up a dozen of them. The more faith you expend, the more power is released. It's an inexhaustible, eternally renewable resource. It's the only power some of these people have.

So the longer you witness it, unless you just don't get into the spontaneous and unexpected, the more you become a part of it. *I* did, and the handlers could tell. They knew before I did what was going to happen. They saw me angling in. They were already making room for me in front of the deacons' bench. As I said, I'd always been drawn to danger. Alcohol. Psychedelics. War. If it made me feel good, I'd do it. I was always up for a little trip. I figured if I could trust my guide, I'd be all right. I'd come back to earth in one piece. I wouldn't really lose my mind. That's what I thought, anyway. I couldn't be an astronaut, but there were other things I could do and be. So I got up there in the middle of the handlers. J.L. Dyal, dark and wiry, was standing on my right; a clean-cut boy named Steve Frazier on my left. Who was it going to

be? Carl's eyes were saying, you. And yes, it was the big rattler, the one with my name on it, acrid-smelling, carnal,
alive. And the look in Carl's eyes seemed to change as he
approached me. He was embarrassed. The snake was all he
had, his eyes seemed to say. But as low as it was, as repul-
sive, if I took it, I'd be possessing the sacred. Nothing was
required except obedience. Nothing had to be given up except
my own will. This was the moment. I didn't stop to think
about it. I just gave in. I stepped forward and took the snake
with both hands. Carl released it to me. I turned to face the
congregation and lifted the rattlesnake up toward the light.
It was moving like it wanted to get up even higher, to climb
out of that church and into the air. And it was exactly as the
handlers had told me. I felt no fear. The snake seemed to be
an extension of myself. And suddenly there seemed to be
nothing in the room but me and the snake. Everything else
had disappeared. Carl, the congregation, Jim — all gone, all
faded to white. And I could not hear the earsplitting music.
The air was silent and still and filled with that strong, even
light. And I realized that I, too, was fading into the white. I
was losing myself by degrees, like the incredible shrinking
man. The snake would be the last to go, and all I could see
was the way its scales shimmered one last time in the light,
and the way its head moved from side to side, searching for
a way out. I knew then why the handlers took up serpents.

There is power in the act of disappearing; there is victory in the loss of self. It must be close to our conception of paradise, what it's like before you're born or after you die.

I came back in stages, first with the recognition that the shouting I had begun to hear was coming from my own mouth. Then I realized I was holding a rattlesnake, and the church rushed back with all its clamor, heat, and smell. I remembered Carl and turned toward where I thought he might be. I lowered the snake to waist level. It was an enormous animal, heavy and firm. The scales on its side were as rough as calluses. I could feel its muscles rippling beneath the skin. I was aware it was not a part of me now and that I couldn't predict what it might do. I extended it toward Carl. He took it from me, stepped to the side, and gave it in turn to J.L.

"Jesus," J.L. said. "Oh, Jesus." His knees bent, his head went back. I knew it was happening to him too.

Then I looked around and saw that I was in a semicircle of handlers by the deacons' bench. Most had returned their snakes to the boxes, but Billy Summerford, Glenn's bucktoothed cousin, still had one, and he offered it to me, a medium-sized canebrake that was rattling violently. I took the snake in one hand without thinking. It was smaller than the first, but angrier, and I realized circumstances were different now. I couldn't seem to steer it away from my belt line. Fear

had started to come back to me. I remembered with sudden
clarity what Brother Charles had said about being careful
who you took a snake from. I studied the canebrake as if I
were seeing it for the first time and then gave it back to Billy
Summerford. He passed it to Steve Frazier, the young man
on my left. I watched Steve cradle it, curled and rattling furiously in his hands, and then I walked out the side door of
the church and onto the steps, where Bobbie Sue Thompson
was clutching her throat and leaning against the green shingles of the church.

"Jesus," she said. "Jesus, Jesus."

It was a sunny, fragrant day, with high-blown clouds. I
looked into Bobbie Sue's face. Her eyes were wide and her
mouth hooked at the corner. "Jesus," she said.

I thought at first she was in terrible pain, but then I realized she wasn't. "Yes. I know. Jesus," I said.

At the conclusion of the service, Brother Carl reminded everyone there would be dinner on the grounds. Most of the
women had already slipped out, to arrange their casseroles
and platters of ham on the butcher paper that covered the
tables the men had set up under the trees. Jim and I waited
silently in line for fried chicken, sweet potatoes, and black
bottom pie, which we ate standing up among a knot of men
who were discussing the merits of various coon dogs they'd

owned. "The next time you handle a snake," Jim whispered, "try to give me a little warning. I ran out of film."

I told him I'd try, but that it was not something I'd be likely to do in the future, or be able to predict even if I did. There was more I wanted to tell him, but I didn't know how, and besides, I figured he knew. We'd lain in a ditch together thinking we were dead men. It was pretty much the same thing, I guessed. That kind of terror and joy.

"This one I had, it was a cur," said Gene Sherbert, a handler with a flattop and a scar. "He treed two coons at the same time."

"Same tree?" one of the other men asked.

"Naw," Gene said. "It was two separate trees, and that fool dog nearly run himself to death going back and forth."

The men laughed. "Was that Sport?" another man asked.

"Sport was Brother Glenn's dog," Gene said, and he turned his attention back to his plate.

I remembered then that Gene Sherbert was the man Glenn Summerford had accused Darlene of running with. I tried to imagine them in bed together — his flattop, her thick auburn hair. Gene was also Brother Carl's cousin. He'd kept the church in Kingston going while Carl did drugs and chased women on the Coast. Where was Brother Carl? I found a trash bag for my paper plate and went off to find him. I still felt like I had not come back all the way from the handling.

My feet were light, my head still encased in an adrenaline cocoon. The air in the oak grove was golden. A breeze moved in the leaves and sent a stack of paper plates tumbling across the grass. On the breeze I heard snatches of a sweet and gentle melody. It was coming from a circle of handlers at the edge of the grove. Some were standing, some leaning against cars, some squatting on their heels in the dirt. As I got closer, I saw that Cecil Esslinder, the redheaded guitar player from Scottsboro, was sitting in the center of the circle. He was playing a dulcimer under the trees.

I stopped and listened. I'd never heard music more beautiful. It was filled with remorse and desire. When it ended, I asked Cecil what song he'd been playing. He shrugged. A hymn about Jesus. I asked how long he'd been playing the dulcimer.

"Never played one before in my life," he said.

His wife, Carolyn, was leaning into the fender of a battered Dodge Dart behind him. "Come on, Cecil," she said. "I want to go. My head is killing me."

Cecil smiled up at me, but he was talking to Carolyn. "You ought to go up and get anointed with oil. Let 'em lay hands on you. Ask for a healing. God'll heal you."

"I know that," Carolyn said. "But you've got to have faith."

"You've *got* faith," Cecil said, still smiling at me.

"My faith's been a little poorly." She took a pill bottle from the pocket of her dress. "I'm putting my faith in here," she said.

Cecil just laughed, and so did the other men. He handed the dulcimer back to its owner and stood up from the grass. "There's something I forgot to tell you," he said to me, although I couldn't even remember the last time we'd talked.

"You have to be careful when you're casting out demons," he said. "An evil spirit can come right from that person into *you*."

That's when it washed over me, the memory of the story I'd written when I was nineteen. "Salvation on Sand Mountain." About a church like the Old Rock House Holiness Church, and two brothers, family men, who pretend to get saved, so they can fake their own rapture, caught up like Elijah in the air, when what they're really doing is running off to live with their girlfriends in Fort Payne. I'd never been on Sand Mountain when I wrote the story, but twenty-five years later, I knew that this was the place. This was the church, in a grove of oak trees, surrounded on all sides by fields of hay. I don't mean it resembled the church in my story. What I mean is that this was the church *itself*.

At the heart of the impulse to tell stories is a mystery so profound that even as I begin to speak of it, the hairs on the back of my hand are starting to stand on end. I believe that the writer has another eye, not a literal eye, but an eye on the inside of his head. It is the eye with which he sees the imaginary, three-dimensional world where the story he is writing takes place. But it is also the eye with which the writer beholds the connectedness of things, of past, present, and future. The writer's literal eyes are like vestigial organs, useless except to record physical details. The only eye worth talking about is the eye in the middle of the writer's head, the one that casts its pale, sorrowful light backward over the past and forward into the future, taking everything in at once, the whole story, from beginning to end.

I found Brother Carl by his pickup truck. He was talking to J.L. Dyal. They'd just loaded the big yellow-phase rattler into the bed of the truck, and they were giving him one last look.

Carl hugged me when I walked up. "I sure am proud of you," he said.

I asked if he was leaving for Georgia already.

"I've got to get back to God's country," he said.

While Carl went to say goodbye to some of the others, J.L. and I stared at the snake in the back of the truck. I told J.L. I just couldn't believe that we'd taken it up.

"It's something, all right," he said.

I asked what it had been like for him.

"It's love, that's all it is," he said. "You love the Lord, you love the Word, you love your brother and sister. You're in one mind, one accord, you're all combined together. The Bible says we're each a part of the body, and when it all comes together . . . Hey!" He whistled through his teeth. "What was it like for you?" he asked.

I didn't know what to say.

It's hard for me to talk about myself. As a journalist, I've always tried to keep out of the story. But look what had happened to me. I loved Brother Carl, but sometimes I suspected he was crazy. Sometimes I thought he was intent on getting himself, and maybe the rest of us, killed. Half the time I walked around saying to myself, "This thing is real! This thing is real!" The other half of the time, I walked around thinking that nothing was real, and that if there really was a God, we must have been part of a dream he was having, and when he woke up . . . *poof!* Either way, I worried I'd gone off the edge, and nobody would be able to pull me back. One of my uncles by marriage was a Baptist minister, one of the kindest men I've ever known. I was fifteen, though, when he killed himself, and I didn't know the whole story. I just knew that he sent his family and friends a long, poignant, and some have said beautiful letter about how he was ready to go meet Abraham, Isaac, and Jacob. I believe he ran a high-voltage line from his basement to a ground-floor bedroom. He put "How Great Thou Art" on the record player. Then he lay down on the bed, reached up, and grabbed the live wire. He left a widow and two sons. My uncle's death confirmed a suspicion of mine that madness and religion were a hair's breadth away. My beliefs about the nature of God and man have changed over the years, but that one never has. Feeling after God is dangerous business. And Christianity without passion, danger, and mystery may not really be Christianity at all.

9

WAR STORIES

———

"Every time you go through one spiritual door," Charles McGlocklin said, "there will be another to go through. Every time you go through one, you'll get stronger, you're led by the Spirit more, the Spirit can reveal things to you and let you know more and more, and the more it can trust you with, the more it will let you have."

During that spring and summer, word had gotten around among the handlers that I was one of them. "He's not only taken up serpents, he's washed my feet, and I've washed his!" Brother Carl would say from the pulpit at churches all along the snake-handling circuit. "This book he's writing is going to spread the gospel to every nation! It's going to reach more people than have been reached by all us snake-handling preachers put together! Why don't you stand up and give your testimony, Brother Dennis!"

And I would. It wasn't so hard once I got the hang of it. I'd just list the things I was thankful for: my family, my health, and the kindness of Carl and Carolyn Porter, and Charles and Aline McGlocklin. I didn't have any stories as spectacular as Anna Pelfrey's, who had been raised from the dead twice by prayer. But I would say that I could feel God moving in my life, and I meant it. Sometimes, I'd even sing. One of the great things about snake-handling services is that even the tone deaf are encouraged to perform.

Some of the younger handlers, who had grown up around snake handling and never known anything else, were probably suspicious of me even then, but the older ones seemed to accept me. They'd lived in the world. They didn't think it so odd that someone from outside the snake-handling family would want to come in and partake.

In May, I drove up to Happy, Kentucky, to persuade Gracie McAllister, an older member of the church in Jolo, West Virginia, to sign a release form so that some video I'd shot at her church could air on *National Geographic Explorer*. Gracie had refused to give her permission by telephone, and I figured she objected on principle to the videotaping of services. But after tracking her down to show her the tape, I discovered she didn't mind being videoed at all. In fact, she had her *own* snake-handling tapes. It wasn't the presence of a camera that disturbed her. She had just been worried that the footage might wind up in the wrong hands. She said that still photographs of services at Jolo had appeared once in *Hustler* magazine.

While we were talking, one of Gracie's sons, D.J., stopped by with his baby daughter. "See her little glass eye?" D.J. said. He set the baby in Gracie's lap and turned her to the light. "See them little blood vessels they put in there? They make them look just like real. Cost over nine hundred dollars."

"Pretty," Gracie said. "I can't tell the difference."

D.J. smiled and crouched on his heels. "It ain't a round eyeball," he said. "More like a contact. We have to take it out every night."

The baby was blond haired and blue eyed and four months shy of her first birthday. She seemed perfectly happy in her grandmother's lap until she glanced at the television screen in the corner of the living room, and then she let out a wail and reached for her daddy. On the screen was a videotape of one of her uncles with a seven-foot cobra draped around his neck.

"She's been seeing so many doctors, she's afraid of people," D.J. explained as he took her back.

But a shadow passed over Gracie's face. "I just haven't been around her enough," she said. "She's forgotten who I am." And then she turned to me: "We handled that cobra for over a year before it died. I wish I'd had it stuffed."

Gracie had been in this thing for more than thirty years. Her first husband had been a snake-handling preacher, and she had tried to keep his church going after he died, but she said she couldn't keep a preacher who believed in the signs. The church at Jolo was just one of the churches that Gracie attended now. Like many of the handlers, she'd drive hours to go to church, often several times a week, accompanied by Muffin, her Shih Tzu pup. Some of the other members of the Jolo church thought Gracie was too worldly, but not because of her red car, exotic dog, or VCR. Many of them also had nice cars and VCR's. In fact, Dewey Chafin, the assistant minister, had a special room in his house where he kept his snakes and video library. Sometimes members of the church would handle in that room and watch themselves on video afterward. No, Gracie was thought too worldly because she believed in going to doctors. She went for treatment of a heart ailment. Sometimes, she even went when she got bit by rattlesnakes. That was the worst part. "They hit me pretty hard over at Jolo for that," she said. "You know, a whole lot of them doctors are against serpent handling."

I told her I bet they were.

Gracie said the last time she was bit by a rattlesnake, the only thing that happened to her was that her heart beat fast.

When she went to bed that night, she told her husband, Ray, that she'd been bit. He asked where and turned on the light. She said, "Now, if I die, give me that test to see what killed me, my heart or the snakebite." Then she went on to sleep. The next morning, she got up, cooked, got dressed, and went to church again.

She also handled fire. I'd never seen anybody do that. Seems like I'd just missed it everywhere I'd gone. It must have been more prevalent in Kentucky than on Sand Mountain, although the Summerfords always kept a propane torch handy just in case. Gracie had her own fire bottle, but she was out of kerosene at the moment. She had a video, though, of herself and others holding their arms and legs in the flame of the kerosene-soaked wick. That's what she was doing one July night after she'd sworn she'd never handle rattlesnakes in July again. She'd been bit the previous two Julys. "I decided I'd just handle fire and drink strychnine that night," she said.

Good idea, I thought. It always pays to be on the safe side.

The problem arose as Gracie tried to handle the fire with her feet. She lost her balance and fell on top of three serpent boxes. "I crawled on my knees and got every one of them serpents out," she said. "My friends said, 'Gracie, you said you wasn't gonna handle serpents tonight,' and I said, 'I wouldn't if I hadn't gotten in the fire.'"

You listen to enough of these stories and you start to feel like you've heard them all before. They seem to have the same architecture and tone. They're war stories. Literally. You can take a look outside Gracie's house and see that right away. Happy, Kentucky, is a dozen miles south of Hazard, a coal mining town in an area that anyone might mistake for a battlefield. The hills have been shaved off, the trees splintered, the ground blasted and pulverized. It's a kind of ugliness that can be achieved anywhere, I suppose, but it's most easily found on the borders where cultures clash, in this instance where the Appalachian hill people have run smack up against contemporary America. The emblem in Hazard is a mountaintop scraped flat for a Holiday Inn with an indoor pool and Jacuzzi. Somebody's always dying or about to die in the stories that grow and flourish in places like these. Firefights, mining accidents, snakebites. It's all the same.

There was the time, for instance, down the road in East Tennessee, when Charles Prince got bit by a rattlesnake. Gracie stayed all night at the house where they took him after the bite. Lying on his deathbed, he continued to handle copperheads and drink poison, she said. It took him awhile to die. Gracie was concerned about him, of course; she'd been praying for him all evening, but she was also concerned that their homecoming services the next day might be "messed up" on account of him getting bit. She said, "Brother Prince, do you care for us going to church tomorrow?"

"Go on, Gracie, go on," he said. "Do everything you can for the Lord. I'll be all right."

Gracie said she told some of the others that they'd have to really pray that they'd be able to get into the Spirit the next day. They'd brought eight or ten boxes of serpents. "And you know," she said, "the Lord got Brother Prince off my mind. We got in the Spirit so good. You ought to see the film." They never could figure out what killed Charles Prince, the venom or the strychnine, Gracie added. She smiled and shook her head.

You see, this can be read as callousness. But so can every good war story. It's part of the form, the way we talk about events that contain too much meaning to be comprehended or too much suffering to be faced head-on. A smile, a shrug. Or a line delivered deadpan. When a handler tells you about somebody's leg that "swole up and burst," or how bad the gangrene smelled, you can't take the grin at the end too seriously. It doesn't mean the storyteller hasn't experienced or felt deeply about what happened. On the contrary, the understatement and the gallows humor is a dead giveaway that something mysterious and wrenching has occurred, is occurring all around us in this case. For this is warfare, spiritual warfare. The tragedy is not the death of a particular snake handler, but the failure of the world to accept the gospel that the handler risked his life to confirm. Or, at least, this is how the handlers seem to see it. Inevitably, they will say of a fallen brother, "At least he died in the Lord." The implication is that a world that rejects Christ is wasting its tears when it mourns a believer who has died of snakebite. Better weep for yourselves, the snake handlers say. Or as Gracie said about a former snake-handling preacher who died in the mines, "He was a good snake handler. Worst thing is he went back on the Lord before he got killed."

The issue is complicated, of course, when the snakebite victim is kin. One of Gracie's sons, Kirby Hollins, is married to a woman whose mother died of snakebite at Jolo. Gracie's youngest son, Sam, started handling when he was fourteen years old. Now twenty-three, he has been bitten four times. "The last time I was bit, I ate four jars of homemade sauerkraut, and it made me feel a lot better," he told me that day in Happy, Kentucky. But even Gracie knows that the sauerkraut might not work the next time. What then?

In snake-handling lore, what's remembered about fatal bites is what the victim said before he passed on to the other side. The last requests seem tailored to produce in the listener an impression of magnanimity and spiritual purpose, tinged with a suggestion of good sportsmanship. When Reece Ramsey was bit and died in 1954, he collapsed into the arms of the evangelist conducting the brush-arbor service and requested that the man's daughter sing "Only One Rose Will Do" at the funeral. The story is that the choir began singing "I'm Getting Ready to Leave This World" as Ramsey died in the evangelist's arms.

Rev. Lee Valentine's last words were, "When you hold my funeral, be sure to use my snakes and handle every one of them over my grave." Valentine, a father of seven, had been bitten at the Old Straight Creek Holiness Church on Sand Mountain in 1955.

No one seems to know what Lloyd Hill's last words were. He had survived the bite he received in Birmingham in 1956, but he died of another bite in Georgia four years later. The preacher at that Georgia church, Charlie Hall, was tried for murder under a tough Georgia anti-snake-handling law, but he was acquitted. Charlie Hall would later die of snakebite himself, at Old Straight Creek in Alabama. He refused to have a fan turned on him or a bag of ice placed on his bite. His last words are reported to be, "If you're gonna do that, you might as well take me to the doctor. That's not faith, boys. If I die, I'm just a dead man."

These are the war stories, redundant, understated, clean. Just war stories. Not meant to frighten, just meant to keep the soldier alert and focused on one thing: them snakes. And in every handler's memory are the stories common to every war: the new guy who got scared and died before anybody could learn his name, and the old master sergeant, veteran of many campaigns, who got careless just once in his life, the time it really counted.

The bites themselves are often not the worst part of spiritual warfare. "I've seen people so demon possessed, they'd crawl on their bellies like snakes," Charles McGlocklin told me once. He also told me about a satanist who had shot a preacher in Huntsville and about the cow mutilations on Sand Mountain that police in Albertville were attributing to satanists with helicopters. A woman Charles knew was fighting a spirit that had been telling her to cut her children's heads off. He said he had heard of another woman who could cause the radio to change stations without even touching it.

And Punkin Brown told me the story of how he and Allen Williams had been asked to cast demons out of a girl in the Tennessee mountains. "We went back up there in this real black holler," he said. "Her mother said she'd walk around with a knife in her hand and talk in two or three voices."

The girl was in a back room when Punkin and Allen got there. Several other people were at the house praying for the girl, too. "They were almost in as bad a shape as she was," Punkin said. "Anyway, the girl come through there, buddy, and all her hair had fell out. She wasn't sick. All her hair had just fell out, and where it had come back in, it was just as white as snow. I'd say she was in her twenties. She had piercing blue eyes. Buddy, she'd send a shiver up your spine."

Nothing much happened, he continued, except that when one of the other visitors asked the girl what she was going to do when the Lord put her in hell, the girl replied: "What're you going to do when he puts *you* there? You belong to me, too." Punkin said he almost fell off his seat when she said that. He and Allen tried to pray for her. "But every time the spirit of God would start to move, them other people would jump up and start speaking some kind of tongue or other, and it'd just kill it out. I told Allen, we're going to have to cast the devils out of those other people before we can do any good for her."

Billy and Joyce Summerford, of the Old Rock House Holiness Church near Macedonia, had their own stories about demon possession. Billy and Joyce lived in a neat little farmhouse behind a collapsed chicken farm outside Section. Billy was telling about a rattler that had bit Gene Sherbert on the foot. "Like to killed him," Billy laughed. "He was so swollen he looked like a toad frog, and he was itching, and the juice was running out of his hands and feet."

"Besides the venom, Gene has an allergy to the venom," Joyce explained. "He breaks out like you would if you had the measles or the chicken pox."

Billy and Joyce looked at each other and smiled. "We throwed him in a tub of water," Billy said. "And then we called this other preacher who'd been through all this before, and he said, 'Now, boys, make sure you don't put him in any water, or he'll die.' " They both laughed.

That Gene Sherbert was a card.

"And then he just got stiff," Billy said. He paused, real serious. "We thought he was dead. But then awhile later, he opened his eyes. He said, 'I believe I need to handle that snake again.' So he did!" And the Summerfords started cackling again.

War stories.

I finally asked if they'd ever cast out any demons.

Billy paused. He stroked his angular chin. He looked out the window where the curtains were blowing in a breeze drawn by the kitchen fan. "We've seen demons come out of people," he said. "One of them looked like the man had been eating chocolate, and it smelled like I don't know what."

"Tell him about that other boy," Joyce said. She had put her hand to her chest, the signal of an unpleasant memory, I supposed.

"Well, some people might not believe this," Billy said.

I assured him I was not one of them.

"Well, we went down to this other boy's house," he continued. "I put my hand on him and asked that demon to leave in the name of Jesus." Billy slapped one of his palms against his knee. "That boy turned flips for two hours, and when that demon came out, it was like a pint of spaghetti, but it had, like, *slather* all around it."

Joyce leaned forward confidentially. "That demon had been in him so long, it called itself David," she said. "I'd never seen one like that, that had a name."

Next time I saw Billy and Joyce Summerford, it was at a Sunday night service at their Old Rock House Holiness Church in Macedonia. After the service, Sister Joyce said, "Well, Billy got initiated."

I asked what she meant.

"He got bit. Copperhead. Friday night."

We were standing at the front of the sanctuary. I looked for Billy in the group of men gathered around the serpent boxes. He looked all right to me, same loose joints, same cowlick. Most of the congregation had already left. The men who had stayed were doing their customary snake trading. One of them would offer a friend a rattlesnake, say, and the friend would reciprocate with a trio of copperheads. They were like women swapping recipes after a church social. At that moment, Charles Hatfield was poking through a serpent box full of copperheads, looking for a big one that Brother Carl Porter had promised him. Gene Sherbert had two rattlesnakes he wanted to pass on to somebody. He had opened the lid to their box, but he was looking over at Charles

Hatfield to see if he'd found the copperhead he wanted. Outside it was storming. Through the open side door, lightning illuminated the trunks of the old oaks that surrounded the church.

"I guess she told you I got bit," Billy said as he walked over to Joyce and me. He rolled up one of his shirtsleeves to reveal an arm swollen and red from the elbow to the wrist. Because of the long sleeves, I hadn't noticed the swelling when Billy had been handling rattlesnakes earlier in the service.

"I had about fifteen serpents laying up here," Billy said, gesturing toward the pulpit. "Brother Carl said, 'Well, don't look like the Lord's gonna move to handle these tonight,' and I just reached up there and got 'em, and one reached around and bit me."

Snakes will do that, I wanted to say.

"The good thing is," Billy continued, "I had a cold and a stomach virus. It stopped that stomach virus." He waited to let that sink in. "I feel like it could have been a reason for me to get bit," he finally said.

I looked down and happened to see that one of Gene Sherbert's rattlesnakes had escaped from its box and was headed across the floor in the direction of my leg. I just stood there in a kind of daze watching its sinuous progress, thinking how pretty it looked. About that time, James Hatfield shouted, "Watch that rattler! Watch that rattler!"

My heart did a double flip. I tried to move, but couldn't. My feet seemed bolted to the floor. The rattlesnake came within an inch or two of my foot before Charles Hatfield managed to get to it with a snake stick and steer it back into its box.

"They got them snakes mad," said one of the women who had stayed behind. "I can smell 'em."

I tried to be nonchalant. "I wonder where he thought he was going," I said to Joyce and Billy. My heart was still pounding, but it was more than fright. I felt like that snake had been a sign. I'd later learn that it was the same snake that would bite Allen Williams up in Tennessee.

Across the road, in a field, animals start to panic — sheep, lions, tigers, all kinds. A machine is coming. Aline and I can see its light moving toward us. We're in a truck. A voice says, "Sorry, I'll have to move this truck," and shoves it. Aline's driving. "Do you know how to drive?" I say. "Not real well," she answers. I take the wheel and steer the truck toward the side of the road. We stop in front of an enormous house. It's filled with people. "What year is this?" I ask. They laugh — it's 1908 or something like that. "Where we live," I say, "it's 1993." They're shocked. It must be a joke, they say. Then the mantel above their fireplace begins to melt or like a mudslide flows downward. Babies and women

are falling in the mud. Aline's in there. I grab her, pull her
out. She's trying to get her baby out. I pull out a baby. It's not
hers. I pull out another — it's Aline's. No, it is Aline.

This is what I'm dreaming when Brother Carl calls after
midnight on a Sunday morning in late July. It's Vicki, not
Aline, in the bed next to me, and we're at home in Birmingham. "Hey," Carl says. "Kirby Hollins got bit. Up in West
Virginia."

"Which one's Kirby?" I ask.

"He's one of Gracie McAllister's boys. She was a Hollins
before her husband died. Kirby's married to Lydia, the organist there at Jolo. You remember him. He's a polite boy, wears
a tie."

I do remember him, but only vaguely. Carl says it was a
four-foot rattler whose fangs went so deep they had to pry the
snake off of him. Kirby is in real bad shape, vomiting blood
and everything. It's especially hard on Lydia because her
mother died of snakebite. Now her husband has been bit.
"You never know what shape somebody's faith's in when
they're handling," Carl says.

I ask him what he means. "Wait on the Lord's about all
you can say. Just wait on the Lord."

I don't know what he means, but I ask him to let me know
how things go with Kirby. He says he will.

I hand the phone back to Vicki. "Who was that?" she asks.

"Carl Porter. One of the guys in West Virginia got bit bad."

"I'm sorry to hear that." She asks me if I knew him well and whether he's likely to survive. I tell her I know which one he is, that's all, and that it doesn't look good. We talk awhile longer, about snake handling, and other things. "You sound different about it," Vicki says. "Have your feelings changed?"

I ask her what she means. She used to be a therapist, and she almost always has reasons for questions she asks. "It just seems that you had reached a point where you really believed in what the handlers were doing."

I tell her I still do, I think. In my way. It's a delicate thing. She knows I've handled. She wants me to be careful. In a little while, she falls back to sleep. I watch her shoulder blades under her gown, the rhythm of her breathing. In the other bedrooms, our daughters are also asleep, and the sound of their breathing is audible, too. Laura has a chest cold. Ashley often talks in her sleep. These are the sounds my household makes. I lie awake listening, thinking things through. The news about Kirby Hollins unnerves me. Terrifies me, in fact. Handling isn't a parlor trick. The rattlesnakes haven't been tampered with or defanged. Brother Carl goes to great lengths to demonstrate that to anyone who dares get close enough to see. And rattlesnakes do not tame, not in the normal sense of

the word. "They might get used to being handled, but they
sure don't get out of the notion of biting you," Dewey Chafin
has told me. "Snakes are unpredictable. They don't care who
you are. They'll bite you. And if they don't kill you, they'll
make you wish you were dead."

When you're under an anointing to handle, you feel certain the snake can't hurt you, but handlers disagree about
the extent of protection the Spirit actually offers. Kentucky
handlers will sometimes talk of a "perfect anointing," during which the handler can't get bit. But Jeff Hagerman, a
friend of Kirby's, told me once that the Kentucky doctrine
was a lie. Jeff had been bitten four times, twice while handling on faith and twice while handling under an anointing. "Just because the Spirit's upon you don't mean you'll
live," he said. He was standing outside the church at Jolo
on a hot summer day, dressed in black from head to foot.
He was wearing a Jesus belt buckle, and his shirt had silver
studs.

Jeff was in his twenties and new to the faith. He originally
came to the church, he said, in order to get his wife and children out of it. But then he became a believer himself. His
own brothers sometimes broke into the church and killed the
snakes in order to keep Jeff away from them. It hadn't done
any good. Jeff said he'd no more give up serpent handling
than he'd give up praying for the sick. He watched his father-

in-law, Ray Johnson, die of rattlesnake bite. They used to drink strychnine together. He paused, as though the memory were pleasant. "I'm not long for this earth," he said.

Lying in bed, thinking of him and Kirby and all the others, I knew that I was in way over my head.

10
THE WIDER CIRCLE:
Elvis Presley Saylor

The week after Kirby Hollins got bit, I ran into Dewey
Chafin at a snake-handling homecoming in Middlesboro,
Kentucky, just west of the Cumberland Gap. We were standing in front of the Church of Jesus Christ, where the service
was reaching the first of many noisy crescendos. It was a
hot, humid day; the church wasn't air-conditioned, and a lot
of us had come outside for fresh air. Dewey looked exactly
the same as he had in Jolo the year before, even down to the
bandage on his hand. "A copperhead bit me on a Saturday,"
he said, "and a week later a rattlesnake bit me on the same
hand." That made bite one hundred and seventeen. Dewey
either had uncommonly bad luck, or good, depending on
whether you thought it was good luck to survive a bite only
to be bit again.

I asked him how Kirby was doing.

Dewey shook his head. "That rattlesnake gave him a hard lick. In thirty seconds, he was down. It took two of us to handle him. He weighs around two hundred pounds."

"That's like dead weight," added one of the Kentucky handlers.

"We laid him on the floor at Barb's house," Dewey continued. "It was Wednesday before he could say anything. Then his eyes rolled back, and he said, 'Goodbye, Dewey, I'm going, I'm going.'"

Dewey seemed amused by this. "I said, 'Where you going, Kirby?' I mean, he couldn't even walk yet. He said, 'To heaven.' I said, 'Oh, you don't want to go there yet.'"

"Maybe he did," the Kentucky handler said.

"Maybe so," Dewey replied with a grin.

The Kentucky handler said his uncle had gotten bit recently by a copperhead. "You know, that copperhead with a skinned place on his back where a motorcycle ran over him?"

Dewey knew the one.

The Kentucky handler was worried because his uncle had gotten bit in the stomach and it was "starting to rot down in there."

About that time, the door of the church opened, unloosening an avalanche of sound, and Brother Carl Porter stepped out. "Y'all come on in here and get you a blessing!" he shouted.

Inside, the sermon was being preached by Brother Bill Pelfrey from Newnan, Georgia. Brother Bill was a big man with a topknot of white hair and a perpetually annoyed look on his face. Earlier in the service, he'd almost been bitten by a little yellow rattler that Punkin Brown said had just been caught the day before and hadn't been prayed over good. As it was being handled by somebody else, the rattler had struck within inches of Brother Bill's waistline. Like everything else, the close call seemed to have annoyed him. His own father had died of snakebite in 1968, and that's what he was talking about when we entered the sanctuary.

"People say, 'Brother Bill, sometimes we see you up there, and you look just like your dad,'" he said.

Amen.

"And the devil speaks sometimes and says, 'Boy, you're gonna *die* just like your dad.'"

No, Lord.

Brother Bill leaned down toward the congregation like he suspected us of insubordination. It was a good crowd, nearly two hundred people, and nearly all waving funeral-home fans with Jesus on the front. He said, "Well, praise the Lord, the way my daddy died is a good way to go! I'd whole lot rather cross over to the other side with a serpent bite than with a bullet in my heart because I was chasing another man's wife!"

Some choice, I thought, but the rest of the congregation said, *That's right! Preach on!*

I'd known Brother Bill since the Scottsboro days, and at
first his no-nonsense, regimental style had put me off. One
time, he said he believed if you didn't handle rattlesnakes, you
were going to hell. That seemed to me to make for a very
small heaven. But despite his theology, he'd grown on me. His
language could be vivid and succinct. "I've seen the Holy
Ghost so strong that you couldn't see the back of the church
for the haze," he would say. And he often called seminaries
"cemeteries" because they were so full of dead men's bones.

Born and raised in Big Stone Gap, Virginia, Brother Bill
had gotten the Holy Ghost in 1966, on his way to Vietnam,
but he hadn't started handling serpents until 1987, after he
retired from the air force. Brother Bill's wife, Anna, carried
the distinction of having died twice. Both times, she was
revived by prayer. "I'll never forget the first time she died, in
our living room," Brother Bill would say. They had a daughter named Diane who worked as a waitress at the Shoney's
in Newnan. She'd sometimes drive the three hours to
Scottsboro after her shift ended so she could sing "In My
Robe of White, I Will Fly Away," one of her daddy's favorite
songs. Diane handled serpents, too, in spite of the fact that a
snake had killed her grandfather before she was born.
Toward the end of my journey with the handlers, she'd get
married, and for reasons best left to that part of the story,
I'd know it was time then for me to move on.

Brother Bill was right in the middle of what I thought was

one of his best sermons ever when a skinny Kentucky handler suddenly leapt to his feet and ran over to a woman sitting
in the third row. He grabbed the back of the pew in front of
her, and his eyes rolled up in his head.

"*Ooooooooohhhh!*" the Kentucky handler said.
"*Mmmmmmmmmm!*" His head snapped back. "*Lalalala,
shhhh!*" And then: "Oh, child, I heard you the first time
that you prayed! When you called out on my name, I said,
surely you do this that I've taught you to do and you'll see
the enemy flee!" His head jerked up and down, and his
mouth went all gooey again. "*Ooooooh! Mmmmmm!
Lalalala, shhhh!* And I say, surely he won't return!" With
these last words, the boy did a flamenco across the floor, his
cheap shoes pounding on the wood.

Amen. Thank God.

"Can you hear what the Spirit has to say?" Bill Pelfrey
asked, cupping his ear with his hand.

But the Kentucky boy wasn't finished yet. "*Ohhhhhhhh,
lalalalala!* Oh, surely I know the trouble, I know the
heartache, and I know the pain that the Wicked One's
caused, but surely I'll come and I'll cut him off without leaving him a single thing!"

Brother Bill seemed perplexed by this last part. "Don't
you come to me with no tricks of the words of the devil," he
said, "or trying to confuse the words of God, because there
is no confusion in the Holy Ghost!"

I didn't know what was going on, and I wouldn't until the service was over and I tracked down the skinny Kentucky boy in the grassy parking lot that sloped down from the church. If anything, the heat and humidity had increased. The handlers' shirts were sticking to their backs as they popped the releases on their car trunks to get to their ice chests.

The boy had just gotten a cup of cold lemonade. His name was Wayne. He had a narrow head, widely spaced eyes, and what looked like the beginnings of a goiter.

"Was that prophecy?" I asked him.

"That was the Lord speaking," he said.

I asked him how he knew.

"The Bible said that when men are led by the Spirit of God, they are the sons of God," he said. "And the son'll know what his father's gonna do."

"Who you think that Wicked One is, Wayne?" a voice asked.

Wayne squinted into the sun, and I turned to see a handsome young man in a mustache and a tropical-looking shirt. He didn't resemble any of the other handlers, although I knew he was one. I'd seen him take up a rattlesnake earlier in the service.

"Who do you think that Wicked One is?" the man repeated. He waved a sweat bee away from his forehead.

Wayne's eyes blinked rapidly. "I don't know, brother," he said.

"Is it anybody in particular?"

"It's a person," Wayne said slowly. "I don't know who it is, but I know somebody's in trouble." He finished his lemonade, excused himself, and went on back up the hill toward the church, where Brother Bill Pelfrey and Brother Carl were coming down the steps, a serpent box in each hand.

The man in the tropical shirt smiled and introduced himself as Elvis Presley Saylor. "That was me he was talking about," he said. "I'm the Wicked One."

"*You're* the Wicked One?" I asked.

He looked me in the eye and said, "That's who they say I am."

The times when I most felt I was closing in on the truth about the handlers, I also felt I was somehow being led by the Spirit. I don't believe it is a conceit to think you are being led by the Spirit. It may be a conceit to say such a thing publicly. But if you accept the idea of a universe set into motion by an intelligent hand, then it seems to me you need to consider the possibility that the hand may still be at work in its movement. Things happen. But chance and coincidence don't mean much to me anymore. Elvis Presley Saylor is an example of what I'm talking about. I believe there was a reason I ran into him that day. It's an idea I never would have entertained a year or two ago. But among the handlers, I'd learned not to dismiss anything as meaningless. Mystery, I'd read somewhere, is not the absence of meaning, but the presence of more meaning than we can comprehend.

I lost Elvis after the service that day in Kentucky. I assume he joined the rest of us at the dinner held outdoors under stretches of bright blue canvas in the backyard of a nearby house, but I didn't see him there. The tables groaned under the fried chicken, potato salad, and field peas. Fleshy red tomatoes. Corn bread burned on the bottom. Fried corn. String beans. Collard greens. Platters layered with thick pink slices of ham. Homemade butter pickles. Olives. Iced tea. Ambrosia and lemon meringue pie for dessert. It was a chance for the handlers from five or six states to swap stories and renew acquaintances. The favorite topic of conversation seemed to be the crazy little yellow rattler that had almost gotten Bill Pelfrey that day. Otherwise, it was just another church social. But for the first time it struck me how small the circle of handlers actually was. At least this circle. By now I'd been to homecomings in Georgia, Alabama, West Virginia, Tennessee, and Kentucky, and I had been seeing the same faces wherever I went: Dewey Chafin, Carl Porter, Bud Gregg, the Summerford brothers, Punkin Brown, Jamie Coots, Gene Sherbert. While the churches themselves are not associational — there is no denomination, for instance, of snake-handling churches, and their beliefs often seem irreconcilably incompatible — the handlers and their families visit each other's churches regularly and even marry into them. The congregations are not connected in any organizational sense, but they are often connected by blood. Bill Pelfrey's daughter, Diane, wound up marrying a cousin of Punkin Brown's. Jimmy Summerford's daughter, Melissa, had married the son of Bud Gregg, pastor of the church in Morristown, Tennessee. Gracie McAllister's son, Kirby Hollins, had married into the Elkins clan. On Sand Mountain, the snake-handling Millers and Mitchells and Hatfields were all tangled up together by marriage. The snake-handling congregations, widely separated by geography, often seem to constitute a series of extended families. Scholars call them "stem families." The Elkins in West Virginia, the Saylors (no relation to Elvis) in Kentucky, the Greggs in Tennessee, and the Mitchells and Summerfords in Alabama. And as in any clan, the outsider, particularly the interloping male, is kept at bay.

I felt oddly detached at the dinner that day. By now, I'd heard all the patterns of small talk, the snake-trading stories, the disguised bravado. Jimmy Summerford invited me to a homecoming at Old Straight Creek on Sand Mountain. He said they hadn't handled there much in recent years, and he and some of the others from Old Rock House in Macedonia were trying to help them out. "I guess they got a little slack after their pastor got bit and died," he said.

"I guess so," I replied.

Verlin Short, of Mayking, Kentucky, began reminiscing about his father, who was out of snake handling for the moment, but might get back in at any time. In particular, Verlin remembered with a certain wistfulness one of the last times he'd seen his father handle. "He had a rattler across his glasses, I don't know how many rattlesnakes he had in his hand, along with some southern copperheads, and he had that green tree viper that just crawled up there on his head like a crown."

Punkin Brown passed along the latest on two famous Tennessee snake-handling preachers, one of whom had quit handling and was living now in what used to be his church. The other had also denied the faith. "He's been married three times," Punkin said, "the last time to a sixteen-year-old girl. He said the Lord told him to do it."

Not even gossip aroused my interest, though, as it once had. Without knowing what I had missed, I was vaguely dissatisfied. Everybody else seemed to be riding on the high of the service. I couldn't figure out why I wasn't. I left the dinner earlier than I'd intended, gassed the car up in Middlesboro, filled myself up with coffee, and that's when I saw him thumbing along the side of the road, Elvis Presley Saylor. The Wicked One. The tropical-print shirt had given him away.

I pulled onto the shoulder, and Elvis hopped in the front. All he had with him was his King James Thompson Reference Bible. He said he was trying to get home to Harlan, Kentucky, and if I wasn't headed in that direction, he'd understand. I told him I wasn't headed in any particular direction, except that I needed to wind up in Akron, Ohio, the next day to do a magazine article. I'd be happy to drop him off in Harlan if he'd show me the way.

Elvis smiled. "I just asked the Lord, if it was his will, that somebody would pick me up and give me a lift," he said.

We rode in silence for a while. Occasionally I'd glance at Elvis to confirm my suspicion that he looked different from the other snake handlers in pretty much the same way that I looked different. His hair was longer, he seemed to still have most of his teeth, and his clothes, although basic, betrayed at least some weakness for the worldly. I couldn't help but ask about his name.

It wasn't something he seemed eager to talk about. "My daddy named me," Elvis said. "He was a bootlegger, worked in the mines. I got five brothers and five sisters, all half. My dad was the type that went with one woman for a while, and then another. I reckon every one of us was named after somebody famous."

Elvis himself had worked in the mines for fifteen years, until an injury forced him to quit. He said he had a pinched nerve in his back and a case of black lung disease. He'd signed up for benefits and hoped a check was coming soon. He'd been a bridge man, a belt man, and a wall builder who sealed rooms so air would flow toward the face of the coal. He'd set pumps, jacks, and timbers. He'd shoveled a lot of coal. But unlike many of the other miners, he'd never taken to drink. "From what I've seen of drinking," he said, "I don't want no part of it."

We were winding through spectacular country, steep green mountains and precipitous ravines. Where the highway bisected the mountains, the cuts revealed layers of gray limestone and black seams of coal.

"I had a kind of bad experience back there," Elvis said, "but you know that. I was jumped on, told not even to talk to you. What they're doing is taking sides in a marital problem that is none of their business."

I asked him what had happened.

"My wife, Brenda, is wanting a divorce," he said. "They're teaching her that since I've been married before, it's fornication, and she's got to get out of the marriage."

Elvis opened the Bible and thumbed through it, as if searching for the appropriate text. The pages were underlined and highlighted in several different colors. Handwritten notes filled the margins. "The Word doesn't back that up," he said, "but they're filling her head with it anyway." The irony, he said, was that his first wife had run off with a snake-handling preacher.

Elvis had an exceptionally quiet voice, but tuned to that East Kentucky dissonance, so that it seemed to come from a broken instrument. "They're saying I'm the devil," he said. "Even Punkin Brown took a fit, almost a fighting fit against me, and I don't even know the man that well."

It didn't surprise me that Punkin Brown's name had come up. There was something dark and brooding about Punkin. He had an admirable knowledge of the Bible, but his sermons, preached in a guttural monotone while he stalked in front of the congregation with a rattlesnake draped over one shoulder, had always struck me as short on grace and long on tribulation. Of all the handlers I'd run into, Punkin Brown seemed to be the one most mired in the Old Testament, in the enumerated laws and the blood lust of the patriarchs. He didn't have much to say about redemption. And he was unpredictable and combative, the handlers' equivalent of a mad monk.

"Punkin prophesied once that I was the god Baal walking in the flesh. He said I was coming in there as a trap for my wife to deceive the church." Elvis shook his head. "I come to find out that he was wanting my wife, and he's married and got kids."

The shadows thrown by the mountains were black and razor-sharp across the roadway. I realized how much I'd always hated this about churches, the inevitable darkness on the underside of any human enterprise. Envy. Bitterness. The division that always seems to doom even the best of intentions. I was guilty of all that, too.

"I didn't even know what Baal was," Elvis said, "and my wife told me to look it up, and I looked it up, and Baal is a stone idol or something. There's also a Baal spirit, of false religion. But I don't prophesy, and I believe in the apostles' teachings, so according to the Word, I couldn't match up to be that false prophet."

He turned his Bible this way and that in the fading light, his restless fingers moving across the page. He was trying to find it, the key word or phrase that could defeat his accusers and reinstate him in the family of faith. All at once the dimensions of Elvis's tragedy struck me. He was an outcast from his own people. He had been prophesied against, driven away, accused of blasphemy and idolatry, of breaking the sacred laws. He was an exile from the only religious establishment this corner of the world had. Like Jesus.

"Not too long ago they prophesied to me that I was a son of God," he said. "Now they're saying I'm the devil. But if you've got the spirit of God in you, you won't be prophesying one thing one day and another thing the next day. The Lord's straight. He's got a map. He doesn't change his mind from day to day. He's the same today and forever."

Amen. I wanted to tell him that I understood what he was going through and that he was right. God would never turn on him the way they had. But who was I to talk? What did I know? And what kind of weird transformation had I been going through? Why did I think the Holy Spirit had a hand in this? Who was I kidding? Had I lost my mind?

"There's a lot of foolishness goes on in serpent-handling churches, but that doesn't change the fact that serpent handling's right," Elvis said. "I've handled eight or nine times. I've drunk the strychnine. When the Spirit of God comes on me, it's like electricity. It doesn't make my hair stand up, but it goes through my body. And the fruits of the Spirit is how you know true love, and that's your evidence of salvation."

Preach it.

"Well, I hope I haven't brought my personal problems into our conversation too much," he said.

I told him he hadn't.

"A lot of people get obsessed with serpents," he added. "They may accept you at first, but if you see something that's not right and mention it, they'll prophesy against you or say you're lost."

I told him I'd remember that. It was nearly dark when we got to the house he still shared with Brenda, although he said he had to sleep in the basement now. "When you pray, pray that God'll work things out for me," he said.

I told him I would.

"If we can't love one another here on earth, there ain't no way we can make it to heaven," he said. "Were you looking for me today, at the dinner?"

I told him I was.

"It was meant to be, then," he said. "I'm glad you came along."

I watched Elvis walk toward the house, his shirt a bright piece of color against an otherwise dark landscape. Then I made a U-turn and retraced the route back through the mountains. The radio stations were few and far between, but occasionally I could pick up snatches of an East Kentucky boy preacher. *There are wells without water,* he said, *clouds that are carried with a tempest; to whom the mist of darkness is reserved forever.* I thought about Elvis, and the way he had been ostracized. What I didn't know was that what had happened to him was about to happen to me. At the time, I just turned the radio off when I got to the interstate that would take me to Akron, the same one that would eventually lead me home.

11

THE WEDDING

My career as a snake-handling preacher was a brief one. It began and ended on a single day in December of 1993, when Vicki and I and photographer Melissa Springer went to a wedding at Carl Porter's church in Georgia, an occasion that seemed to arouse all the passion, violence, and mystery that lay at the heart of snake handling itself. It was a little over two years after Glenn Summerford had put a gun to his wife's head and forced her to stick her hand into a cage filled with rattlesnakes.

In those two years, I had been drawn by chance and inclination into a close relationship with the handlers. I had come to admire them and to respect their faith. In the process, I had even taken up serpents myself. It was perhaps a measure of the intimacy I shared with the handlers that I had also come to see their faults. They surely saw mine. My faith had grown;

so had my doubts. But the mystery of snake handling had deepened. For the mystery was not *how* the handlers did what they did, or even how it *felt*. The mystery was *why,* and toward what particular outcome.

The handlers say they do it in order to confirm the Word. Jesus says that believers shall take up serpents. Somebody's got to do it, or the Word is found to be a lie. The handlers insist they're the ones. But that explanation only scratches the surface of motivation, and in looking at motivation, I understood I had become my own subject. Why had *I* taken up serpents? I knew that I had a need to experience ecstatic worship, an addiction to danger, and a predictable middle-age urge to find out who my people were. But still, the answer seemed incomplete. I turned again to the questions I was asking. What motivated the handlers to do what they did, and what would happen next in their lives as a result? Suddenly I realized those were the same questions I posed about characters in stories. And the answers could never be found outside the story, but only within. I was in a story, and the story I was in had no predictable end. But it had to end somewhere, sometime. I should have seen the end coming. The story had begun with a man trying to kill his wife. It made sense that it would end with a wedding. Then I would know what all this meant.

It was to be the first wedding ever held in the relatively new sanctuary of The Church of the Lord Jesus Christ in

Kingston, Georgia. Halfway between the mill towns of Cartersville and Rome, Kingston looked as though it had once been prosperous. Now it was little more than a whistle-stop fronted by a row of abandoned brick buildings, among them one that had housed the Famous People's Opry. The only businesses that appeared to be open in Kingston on the day of the wedding were an establishment that manufactured cement lawn statuaries, a gas station, a video arcade, and Margo's Groceries, home of a half border collie and half Australian shepherd named Worm.

The bride, Diane Pelfrey, twenty-one, a former waitress at the Shoney's restaurant in Newnan, Georgia, was set to marry Steve Frazier, twenty-four. Diane was a third-generation handler. Her paternal grandfather had died of snakebite before she was born, and both of her parents took up serpents. Her father, Bill Pelfrey, had preached the gospel with signs following at revivals and homecomings all over the South. He spoke in tongues, healed the sick, and occasionally drank strychnine with no obvious ill effects. Diane's mother, Anna Pelfrey, had died twice and been revived by prayer, once on the shoulder of an interstate near Big Stone Gap, Virginia, and once in the family's living room.

Steve, on the other hand, was relatively new to handling. He'd been introduced to it two years earlier by his uncle, John Brown, Sr., and his cousin, the legendary Punkin Brown of Newport, Tennessee. Steve's parents, though, were Catholic and lived on Michigan's upper peninsula. They had never handled poisonous snakes or drunk strychnine. Steve's mother, Nancy, had never even been to Georgia before. She told me this moments before the service started, when I saw her standing outside the church, deduced her identity, and introduced Vicki and myself.

Nancy Frazier was an attractive woman about my age. She appeared serene and composed. Only her hazel eyes gave her away. They were the eyes of a woman who is imagining how she will survive a catastrophe that has not yet begun. "I'm concerned," she said to me in a level voice. "I'm praying about it." She said this would be her first Holiness church service, and she had not, until the day before her son's wedding, met her future daughter-in-law. She already had lost one of her four sons, stabbed to death by hitchhikers two and a half years before. Now she feared she was losing another son, to a family of snake handlers.

But she smiled when Punkin Brown, dressed in a tux, came out of the church to escort her inside. Punkin was not only her nephew, but her son's best man. It must have given her pause. But she took the snake handler's arm anyway and bravely disappeared into the church.

Brother Carl was proud of his church, and he had reason to be. Nothing could have been further removed, in snake-handling circles at least, from Glenn Summerford's con-

verted service station in Scottsboro than Carl Porter's white
masonry church in Kingston. It comfortably sat more than
two hundred worshipers on oak pews with sky blue cushions, each pew adorned with crosses and brass plaques
engraved with the names of donors, including Aunt Daisy,
the prophetess. The building had central heat and air, a water
fountain in the vestibule, and spacious bathrooms off either
side. The basement had been partially finished, as had the
old sanctuary next door, to provide bedrooms for visiting
handlers. And the whole complex was fully paid for. The
place looked particularly inviting decked out in pink roses
for the wedding. A slanting afternoon light fell across the
pulpit and prayer rail. It looked more like a Presbyterian
meeting house in New England than a snake-handling church
in a crumbling Southern mill town.

Having seated the groom's mother, Punkin greeted Vicki
and me just inside the door. He kissed me on the cheek, the
traditional holy kiss, and reminded me that he and Steve
were cousins. When he started to escort Vicki down the aisle,
we told him we were waiting for Melissa, who had gone into
the women's bathroom to take photos of the bride getting
dressed.

Punkin chatted with us awhile. He said he had driven his
aunt's car down from Tennessee for the ceremony. Nancy
had told him not to take any snakes in the car with him, but

he said, "If I don't, I don't go." Out of respect for Nancy, no snakes would be in evidence during the wedding. They'd be there, though, that night for the regular service, which the bridal parties had been invited to attend. "I don't have to bring my snakes every time," Punkin said. "But if somebody tells me not to, I'll sure bring them then."

Punkin had introduced Steve to Diane, he said, and he thought their marriage would be a fine and holy affair. He and his own wife, Melinda, had been married eleven years. They'd met at a homecoming in 1982, when Punkin was eighteen and Melinda fifteen, and now they had four children, including a set of three-year-old twins. Punkin remembered the first time he had seen Melinda. "She was speaking in tongues and handling a big rattlesnake. I told Daddy, 'I'm gonna marry that girl.'"

He excused himself then to seat the other guests.

That's all I knew about Punkin's own marriage, but Carolyn Porter said she disapproved in general of the way the Tennessee handlers treated their wives. "I just don't like the way they boss their women around," she said. She'd tried to talk Diane out of marrying Steve for that very reason, not because she had anything against Steve personally, but because they'd be living among what she and Gracie McAllister called "them old Tennessee." No handlers, Carolyn and Gracie said, were more strict in their attitudes

about the roles of men and women than those from Tennessee. Some of them didn't even believe in men and women
shouting together during a service. The women did their
shouting on one side of the church. The men did theirs on
the other. And the idea of a woman preaching the gospel
was heresy, pure and simple, in Tennessee.

When Brother Carl saw me, he also greeted me with a
holy kiss. He was a little nervous, what with it being the first
wedding in the new building, but he was just happy to see
we'd made the trip.

"Come on and get you a seat up front," he said to me
and Vicki. "You ain't never seen a snake-handling wedding,
have you?"

We shook our heads, afraid to consider what he had in
mind.

"Well, I'll tell you a secret," he said. "It ain't no different
from any other kind."

The crowd was modest, mostly family, and just a dozen
or so handlers outside that. Carolyn Porter was there, and
Charles and Aline McGlocklin. It was a strange and wonderful sight, the male handlers dressed up in tuxes and suits
and ties, a way they'd never be in regular church. Melissa
still hadn't appeared, so Vicki and I sat in the middle, next
to the aisle, with Charles and Aline and Aline's youngest
son, Matthew, to our right. Aline took Vicki's hand. It had

been months since they'd seen each other. I smiled at
Charles, and he gave me a comical look. Our friendship with
the McGlocklins had been brief but intense, and like many
unlikely friendships, it appeared destined to last.

When the families had all been seated on the appropriate
sides of the aisle, the ceremony began. The pianist played the
traditional wedding march. The bride, wearing white, entered
on the arm of her father, Brother Bill Pelfrey. Diane had lux-
uriant, waist-length hair, and considerable poise. She smiled
confidently at the friends she passed. The groom, who stood
between Punkin Brown and Brother Carl, looked pale and
wild eyed, like a startled hare. Carl asked who gave this
woman in marriage. Brother Bill replied, "Her mother and I."
Then he delivered Diane to her maid of honor and slid into
the pew next to his wife.

Brother Carl rocked forward on the balls of his feet, as
officious and ecclesiastical as a snake-handling preacher can
be. He read the passage from Matthew in which the sacra-
ment of marriage is described as separate flesh becoming
one, and then asked if anyone had objections to the union,
and if not, to forever hold their peace. The church was silent,
so Brother Carl continued with the vows. The phrase *as
long as we both shall live* had a particular resonance that day,
given the fact that Diane and Steve intended to continue handling rattlesnakes and copperheads in their new life together.

But Brother Carl had been right. It was a perfectly normal wedding. More tasteful than most, as a matter of fact, simpler, I think. The single detail that set the wedding apart occurred in the moment after Carl had pronounced the couple man and wife, and they kissed each other for what they said was the first time. Ever. For this reason, it was a longer and more involved kiss than I was accustomed to seeing at weddings, and I hoped they'd both liked it well enough. The stakes, after all, seemed awfully high.

After the reception in the basement, with a cake made by Sister Jane Collier and punch served up by other women from the church, the couple left under a shower of rice. The usual pranksters had been at work on the car. "I got me a good Georgia woman" was scrawled in shaving cream on one side. Bill Pelfrey, the father of the bride, took one glance at the car and said, "God, they look like a bunch of Tennessee trash."

It was what happened after the wedding that caused the day to veer off in a new direction and reverberate like a tuning fork. Vicki and I and Charles and Aline were standing outside the church after all the guests had left. Melissa had dismantled her camera gear and was stowing it back in the van. We were going to grab dinner before the regular service later that night, and we had asked the McGlocklins to join us.

We'd assumed they were staying, and we were surprised when Charles said they weren't.

"I just don't think I can make it through the service," he said. "My neck's hurting me too bad."

I knew what an ordeal Charles had been through with his neck, but it seemed odd that he would have ridden all this way from New Hope, a three-hour drive, only to turn back now, before the snake-handling service had even begun. Months later, Charles would tell me his other reason for not staying. "The Lord allowed me to see the spirits in the church during that wedding," he said. "I knew what was going to happen to you, and I just didn't want to have to watch you go through it."

But if he'd told me at the time, I wouldn't have believed him. I had my own premonition about the service. I saved it, though, until Vicki, Melissa, and I had driven the seventeen miles from Kingston into Rome. It was a foggy evening, and the road was nearly deserted. The land along that stretch had always seemed desolate to me, but never as much as it did then, despite the hope I nursed.

We went to a popular chain restaurant in Rome, one of those places that specialize in baby back ribs and honey mustard dressing. I waited until we had finished eating, and then I told Vicki that she was going to get a blessing that night at the service. She asked what I meant. I didn't exactly know myself, but I had a feeling that without the girls there, she might find it easier to give herself to the moment. There was something special in store for her. I knew that, but I couldn't put my finger on what it was.

"All I want," she said, "is for Aunt Daisy to lay hands on me."

Melissa and I laughed.

"I'm serious," Vicki said. "I've been watching her. Have you seen what she does with her hands? It's like she's fighting her way through webs to get to the Spirit. And when she gets there, it's as though she's touched something alive. I can't take my eyes off her."

"Neither can I," Melissa said. "But she doesn't like to have her picture taken."

We hadn't seen Aunt Daisy at the wedding. The last time we'd seen her during a service, Brother Carl had preached standing on top of the pulpit, and Aunt Daisy had tried to climb it from the altar side. After the service, our younger daughter, Laura, had said, "Didn't you see what that woman was drawing with her hands?"

"Where?" we asked.

"In the wood," Laura said. "She was drawing a cross with a snake wrapped around it."

The fog on the way back to Kingston was heavy, and I was so focused on the road, I forgot about the blessing Vicki was going to receive. She reminded me, though, as we pulled up the driveway to Brother Carl's church, that the blessing she wanted was to have Aunt Daisy lay hands on her.

Aunt Daisy showed up at the service, all right, but she was seated at the front of the congregation. She'd never met Vicki, and it looked like she was already lost in the Spirit. Her fingers seemed to be plucking invisible threads from the air. The rest of the crowd filtered in slowly. Among the last to arrive were the newlyweds and their parents, the Pelfreys and the Fraziers. Steve's mother, Nancy, had told us she probably wouldn't come to the service, and I was pleased she'd had a change of heart. It's never a mistake to face one's fears, I reasoned, and I hoped that, out of courtesy, Steve and Diane wouldn't handle that night. I knew I wasn't going to. I didn't feel the craving. Instead, as I thumbed through my Bible, I felt something similar, but oddly reversed, as though the urge were not to step off the ledge, but to step up onto it. It was a calm and secure impression of well-being that kept building, but I didn't know toward what, until Brother Carl stopped in the aisle, pushed his glasses up on the bridge of his nose, and said, "Are you gonna preach tonight?"

Unlike some of my friends growing up, I had never, ever, wanted to be a preacher, not even when I thought I might go to college at Asbury Theological Seminary in Wilmore, Kentucky. A number of older boys from our church in East Lake had decided to go to Asbury, a Methodist school. I looked up to them and almost followed in their footsteps. They were extraordinary young men — sober, reliable, and possessed of a social conscience, a rare thing, it seemed to me, in the white neighborhoods of Birmingham in the early 1960s. Only one of these Asbury boys actually became a minister, I believe, but out of the others would eventually come a doctor, a dentist, a professor of religious studies, and a church youth director. In the summers between academic years, they'd do missionary work overseas or in the mountains of eastern Kentucky, where they lay preached at churches without indoor plumbing or electricity. I particularly remember the slides of Costa Rica that one of them, Glenn Truitt, showed during a Sunday night worship service. The images were grainy and out of focus, but the country they approximated, with its volcanoes and brilliant birds, struck me as terribly exotic and remote. I craved adventures of any sort and resolved to go to Costa Rica some day, although I had no idea it would be as a journalist, or that I would have to get there by way of the wars in El Salvador and Nicaragua first.

The Asbury boys were on to something I wanted, but however much I admired them, I went my own way. I didn't go to seminary in Kentucky: I attended the University of Virginia, instead. Mine was the last group at Virginia to wear coats and ties to class, the last to be exclusively male.

My mother had hoped I would become a doctor. My father had said that all work, if honest, was honorable. The only advice he gave was that I should do something in life I enjoyed, which was the best advice I ever received. To say that I enjoy writing, though, is like saying I enjoy having fingers and toes. It's difficult to imagine life without them.

Of all the things I might have become, I had never wanted to be a preacher, but I became one that evening in the middle of December when Carl Porter stopped in the aisle, looked me over once good, and asked if I was going to preach.

I shrugged and told him I was.

It's difficult for me to recall now the sequence of events or the exact words. I remember that the service began in customary fashion, and that the snakes came out early, but not very many of them. The boxes were kept out of sight behind the altar, and the men who did handle seemed careful to do it behind the plane of the pulpit and prayer rail. The idea must have been to make a good impression on Steve's parents and the other guests from the wedding. But the restraint had a curiously paradoxical effect that became apparent only when Brother Carl himself began to preach. After addressing his preliminary remarks to the Tennessee brethren lining the deacons' bench, Brother Carl came down into the congregation, citing scripture from memory as he descended.

"You can't do both!" he shouted. "You can't walk in the flesh and walk in the Spirit!" Melissa followed him unobtrusively with her camera. She wasn't using a flash, and she was dressed in a style befitting a Holiness woman — an ankle-length black dress, uncut and unadorned hair, a blouse buttoned modestly at the neck. But there was one thing about herself that she could not disguise. Her husband and children weren't by her side. She was a hundred and fifty miles from home on a Saturday night, and she was at work. At one point, Carl was preaching directly to Junior McCormick, who was sitting on the first pew in his red and white plaid pants, his elbows on his knees and his head nodding with every amen he uttered. Carl patted him tenderly on the shoulder. "God'll affirm you in that!" he said. "In Jesus' name, He will!" Then he looked up and came face to face with Melissa. He suddenly seemed not to know her. His customary bashfulness gave way to a humor I can only describe as sexual discomfort. It was as though her camera had finally caught him naked. His cheeks reddened. His jaw set. He pointed his finger in Melissa's face. He was glaring at her, and the sermon that suddenly poured out of his mouth was a diatribe about the necessity for women to stay in their place. "It's not godly for a woman to do a man's job!" he said. "To wear a man's pants! Or cut her hair like a man does his! It doesn't please God to go on like that, acting like Adam was made

out of Eve's rib instead of the other way around!" He
wouldn't let up on her, not even to pace.

Melissa kept on working, bobbing to get the best shots.

"A woman's got to stay in her place!" Carl shouted. "God
made her for a helpmate to man! It wasn't intended for her
to have a life of her own! If God had wanted to give her a
life of her own, he'd have made her first instead of Adam, and
then where would we be!"

I don't know what Carolyn Porter was thinking, but I
could feel Vicki stiffen beside me. Carl was directing his
comments to Melissa, but Vicki knew they were intended for
her as well. I was embarrassed, for Melissa's sake, for Vicki's,
but mainly for my own. I'd told her she was going to receive a
blessing from the service that night, and it looked like she
would receive just the opposite. And finally, of course, I was
disappointed with Carl. He had always been so gentle and
encouraging. He *knew* better than that. I thought he was
doing it on purpose to humiliate us. But I couldn't figure out
why. This was a side of him I'd never seen before. I thought
the sermon would never end. But finally Carl seemed to come
to his senses. I wondered if he would remember everything
that he had said. He stepped back toward the pulpit, told a
few self-deprecating stories about baldheaded preachers,
including one about children who were eaten by bears
because they'd made fun of Elijah's pate. Then he invited

more songs and testimony from the congregation, as though the message he'd just delivered had been his usual fare. At the pulpit, though, he turned and came up short, as if he had just remembered an unpleasantness. "Brother Dennis," he said into the microphone. "Why don't you come up here and preach?"

The wind bloweth where it listeth, and thou hearest the sound thereof, but canst not tell whence it cometh, and whither it goeth: so is every one that is born of the Spirit.

I took a deep breath and glanced at Vicki. She and I, at least, were of one accord. I walked down the aisle as I'd done many times before, to testify, to sing, to lay on hands, to take up serpents. When I stepped up onto the platform, I looked once at the congregation. They were hushed and attentive, even the teenage boys with slicked-back hair and unbuttoned shirts. I took the microphone from its stand and slung the cord out so I'd have slack to move around. Then I went to each of the brethren on the deacons' bench. I shook hands with Bill Pelfrey, Jamie Coots, and the rest. I gave Steve Frazier, the new husband, a hug. He'd handled beside me at Macedonia, and I had always, for that reason, held a special affection for him, and for Diane. Against the wall behind the pulpit sat Punkin Brown, his eyes hooded and dark. I had an unsettling premonition that if Punkin survived the serpent bites and lived to middle age, his face might wind up resembling Glenn Summerford's, so I passed him by with only a nod and lay my hand instead on the head of Billy Lemming, Brother Carl's lean and mysterious guitar player. And then I came face to face with Carl. He was sitting in a folding metal chair with his hands on his knees, a man who had been generous and fatherly to me, and recommended me to his congregation. I couldn't help but smile at him. What was about to happen had been ordained. I think we both knew it. I think we were both savoring that fact.

"I love to testify," I said into the microphone, "but I've never preached before. I just want you to know that I submit myself to your authority, Brother Carl. You're the pastor of this church, and if I step out of the Word, I want you to tell me." He smiled back and nodded. He would.

The choice of text was simple — the chapter the handlers believed so deeply, they were risking their lives to confirm it. "Let's look at Mark 16," I said.

"Amen," Carl replied. He was pulling for me. I looked at the congregation again. They seemed remote and unfamiliar to me now, someone else's family reunion. I couldn't pick out Vicki or Melissa among them.

"It was after they had crucified Jesus," I said, "and some of the women who had stayed with him through it all came down to the tomb to anoint his body with spices. Am I in the Word?" I looked over to Brother Carl.

"You're in the Word," Carl said.

Amen, the congregation answered.

"But the stone had been rolled away from the tomb," I said, "and a man in white, an angel, was sitting there, and the angel said to the women: 'He's not here. He's risen.' Am I in the Word?"

"Amen," Carl said. "You're in the Word."

"I'm in the Word," I repeated, and I moved along the platform like I'd seen Carl do so many times. "And who did Jesus appear to first after his resurrection?"

"The eleven," Carl said.

I turned back to him. "No. He didn't appear first to the eleven." And I walked slowly across the platform again, heading straight for Carl's son Virgil, who was standing by his drum set, sticks crossed in front of him. "He appeared first to Mary Magdalene!" I said, and I drove each word in the direction of Virgil's chest with my finger. "A woman out of whom he had cast seven devils!"

There was no amen.

I whirled back around and faced the congregation again. "The angel had told her to tell the disciples that Jesus was risen, but she was afraid, and she didn't do it. So Jesus himself appeared to her, and when she told the disciples that he had risen, none of the men believed her!"

I was waiting for an amen, which still hadn't come. "*That's* when Jesus appeared to the eleven and *upbraided* them for their unbelief!"

"Amen," Carolyn Porter, Carl's wife, finally said.

I knew I was in the Word now. It was close to the feeling I'd had when I'd handled. "Mary Magdalene was the first person to spread the news of the risen Christ!" I shouted. "She was the first evangelist, and the men didn't even believe her! So when we start talking about a woman's place, we better add that a woman's place is to preach the gospel of Jesus Christ! In Him there is no male or female, no Greek or Jew!" And I spun on Carl. "Am I in the Word?"

"No," Carl said. "You're not in the Word."

"Are you telling me I'm out of the Word?"

"Yes. You're out of the Word." He smiled. It was a smile of enormous satisfaction and relief. At last, we had reached the end of our story, his eyes seemed to say.

I looked back at the congregation. No help there. I was confused. I'd never heard the place so quiet. Anna Pelfrey sat with her feet crossed at the ankles, her hands folded in her lap as though she hadn't heard a word. Some of the men were looking at the floor. Others were stretched out with their arms on the back of the pew. They seemed suddenly curious about the ceiling. Only the teenage girls were animated, heads bent toward one another, whispering furiously, but without a sound.

"Well, if I'm out of the Word," I said, "I'd better stop preaching." My heart was beating fast, and I could feel the blood in my cheeks. I put the microphone back in its stand and walked slowly off the platform and down the aisle. Nobody would look me in the eye except Nancy Frazier, the mother of the groom. She was smiling and pointing to the pew in front of her, the one I was headed for. That's when I saw that Aunt Daisy had moved from the front of the congregation to our pew in the middle, where she was sitting next to Vicki and laying hands on her.

Aunt Daisy had put her pale forehead up against Vicki's chin. Her hands were in Vicki's hair, and then on her forehead, her shoulders, her neck. "You young people are right," she was crooning. "I don't have much time left, but in the time I've got, I'm going to spread the gospel." It was what Vicki had wanted, the blessing I knew she would receive. I slid into the pew beside her, and Vicki continued to sit erect, her eyes closed, while Daisy made over her. The church was silent except for Daisy's warbling voice.

Punkin Brown suddenly leapt to his feet and wrenched the microphone from its stand. "You know, I was supposed to preach tonight, and I had me another sermon in mind." He said this with disdain, as though he hated to waste valuable time on matters as transparent as the ones I'd raised. "But if we can't stand on sound doctrine, boys, we might as well not stand at all."

Amen.

Punkin bent down, unclasped the lid of a serpent box, and brought out a big yellow-phase timber rattler, which he slung across his shoulder like a rope. *"Haaagh,"* he said. It sounded like steam escaping from an underground vent. With the snake in tow, he started strutting across the front of the sanctuary, bent nearly double, his face contorted and red. "If we can't stand on sound doctrine, boys, we might as well give this thing up. *Haaagh.*

"There are people," Punkin said, "who preach a false doctrine, that women can hold authority over men in a church. *Haaagh.* It's the preaching of false prophecy, boys, of the ungodly, the unholy, the profane. *Haaagh.* The whoremonger and them that defiled themselves with mankind. *Haaagh.* God's not in it, boys, and if we pay it any mind, we're as lost as them that give it. *Haaagh.* We might as well deny the whole Word!"

I glanced at Vicki, and she smiled back.

"Oooooh!" he groaned. And his heels beat out a rhythm on the floor as he danced across the platform. *"Haaagh!"* And he flung the rattlesnake back and forth like a trunk. He wiped his forehead with it. He let it brush his lips. *"Haaagh.* Just let them do this," he said, "and we'll see who the Spirit speaks through! *Haaagh.* They're deceivers, boys, Ahab and Jezebel, with her painted face and gold hoops in her ears! *Haaagh.* They wanted the vineyard of Naboth, boys, they killed him and stole it for themselves! And you know what

the Word says about them. *There was none like unto Ahab, which did sell himself to work wickedness in the sight of the Lord, whom Jezebel his wife stirred up.* But the enemy's defeated, boys. *In the place where dogs licked the blood of Naboth shall dogs lick thy blood, even thine.*"

Punkin came to a stop at the spot where Brother Carl had harangued Melissa. There, Punkin caressed the rattlesnake as though it were a part of himself before he caught my eye in the congregation. "It's a lie, Dennis!" he said. "There's no truth in it! It's a sin!"

It was odd for me to see Punkin this way, so grotesque and funny looking, with his shirttail out and a big rattlesnake draped over his shoulder. He was just a child, I thought, an overgrown snake boy like myself.

When Punkin had finished, it was Jamie Coots's turn to prophesy along the same lines. He was still recovering from a severe rattlesnake bite, and so carried a certain weight of moral authority. By the time he finished, it was after nine o'clock. I caught Melissa's eye and nodded toward the door. She was ready, for sure. We'd have to get up and walk out in order to be back in Birmingham before midnight, and that's what we did. But before we left, I stood and explained the reason we were leaving, that we had to get home to be with our children. I thanked Brother Carl and the congregation for letting us visit with them again.

"Please pray for us," I said.

There were nods of assent from the congregation. Carl smiled and bobbed as he usually did. "We appreciate you and love you, Brother Dennis. You and Sister Vicki and Melissa and Jim."

It was as though nothing had happened, but of course everything had. I knew it could never be the same with the handlers. I had found my people. But I had also discovered that I couldn't be one of them, after all. Knowing where you come from is one thing, but it's suicide to stay there. A writing teacher of mine once told me to live in his house as long as I could. He didn't mean his actual house, but the house of fiction he'd made. The only thing he asked was that when I left, I'd leave for good, and that I'd burn the house down. That was exceptionally good advice, and I believe Carl Porter had given it, too. I think he knew what he was doing in releasing me back to the wider world. At the height of it all, after Macedonia, I had actually envisioned myself preaching out of my car with a Bible, a trunkload of rattlesnakes, and a megaphone. I had wondered what it would be like to hand rattlesnakes to my wife and daughters. I had imagined getting bit and surviving. I had imagined getting bit and not surviving. I had thought about what my last words would be. It sounds funny now. It wasn't always funny at the time.

The day after the wedding, I would talk to Carl on the phone. He'd not mention Melissa or Punkin, but rather say he'd been worried about what had happened at the service the night before. He said he hadn't slept well, worrying about us.

"The church I repented in," he explained, "had a woman pastor over it, but I don't believe that way now. I'm like Paul. I suffer a woman not to teach. And a woman can't be a deacon."

There was nothing peculiar or odd about Carl's views. The majority of ministers in our own Southern Baptist Convention probably felt the same way about women in the church. So I didn't tell him that Vicki was already a deacon in our home church in Birmingham. I just told him, truthfully, that she had gotten a blessing out of the service.

"I saw that," he said in the soft voice I'd come to love. "You know, the Lord led Daisy back there to her."

On that, we were both agreed.

It's been several months since I've talked to Carl. Occasionally I get a call from Charles and Aline McGlocklin, though. The theme of these conversations is that they knew what was going to happen that night after the wedding and couldn't bear to watch. They knew we'd gotten hurt in Kingston, but that such injuries could strengthen one's faith.

"I've been hurt before, many times, Brother Dennis," Charles says. "Let me tell you, the bite of the serpent is nothing compared to the bite of your fellow man."

It's sad, in a way. I wish I could assure the Porters and the McGlocklins and all the others that we can be friends as long as we like, but that I won't be taking up serpents anymore. I refuse to be a witness to suicide, particularly my own. I have two daughters to raise, and a vocation in the world.

When we got into the van that night for the long ride home, Melissa said, "I've got all the shots I need." That was all that was said for a long while, until after we'd stopped in Rome for ice cream. Then it all began to tumble out. Vicki said she'd felt sad and hurt during the service. Melissa ran her fingers through her wild blond hair and said it had all seemed painfully familiar to her, but still, she was baffled by Carl's words. He had always been so gentle. It had been worse on her than on us, of course. Melissa had taken the brunt of Carl's wrath, and because her method as a photographer was to merge with her subjects, Carl's sermon had been a personal blow.

In ways, though, it had to have happened the way it did. Melissa and Jim had often taken turns behind the camera. If Jim, rather than Melissa, had been there to photograph the wedding, Brother Carl might not have had a focal point for his message. We might have been spared the night's discomfort, but we wouldn't have known how the story would end. And stories have to end. Endings are the most important

part of stories. They grow inevitably from the stories themselves. The ending of a story only seems inevitable, though,
after it's over and you're looking back, as I am now. And in
retrospect, I can tell you the dispute after the wedding was
not about snakes, or about the role of women in the church.
It was about the nature of God.

The highway from Rome crossed the mountains twice,
once as it entered Alabama and then again fifty miles north
of Birmingham. Those last miles into the city were lonely
and dark, but gradually the traffic along the interstate picked
up. First there were the tractor-trailer rigs, and then the vans
with children asleep in the back. And soon we were being led
back into the city by a river of light, through suburbs and
neighborhoods that became increasingly familiar until I realized the elevated highway was taking us above East Lake,
the old neighborhood where I had grown up not knowing
who my people were. *It's late afternoon at the lake. The turtles are moving closer to shore. The surface of the water is
undisturbed, an expanse of smooth, gray slate. Most of the
children in my neighborhood are called home for supper by
their mothers. They open the back doors, wipe their hands
on their aprons and yell, "Willie!" or "Joe!" or "Ray!" Either
that or they use a bell, bolted to the doorframe and loud
enough to start the dogs barking in backyards all along the
street. But I was always called home by my father, and he*

didn't do it in the customary way. He walked down the alley all the way to the lake. If I was close, I could hear his shoes on the gravel before he came into sight. If I was far, I would see him across the surface of the water, emerging out of shadows and into the gray light. He would stand with his hands in the pockets of his windbreaker while he looked for me. This is how he got me to come home. He always came to the place where I was before he called my name.